ROYAL COURT

The Royal Court Theatre presents

THE ACID TEST

by ANYA REISS

First performance at The Royal Court Jerwood Theatre Upstairs, Sloane Square, London on Friday 13 May 2011.

JERWOOD
NEW PLAYWRIGHTS
Supported by the Jerwood Charitable Foundation

Principal Sponsor

Coutts

THE ACID TEST

by Anya Reiss

in order of appearance
Dana **Vanessa Kirby**
Ruth **Phoebe Fox**
Jessica **Lydia Wilson**
Jim **Denis Lawson**

Director **Simon Godwin**
Designer **Paul Wills**
Lighting Designer **Malcolm Rippeth**
Sound Designer **Nick Manning**
Casting Director **Amy Ball**
Assistant Director **Eleanor Fogg**
Production Manager **Tariq Rifaat**
Stage Managers **Luke Girling, Susan Ellicott**
Costume Supervisor **Iona Kenrick**
Scenic Artist **Bethany Ann McDonald**
Set built by **RCT Stage Dept**
Set Painters **Hayley Kasperczyk**
Furniture Upholstery by **David Young**

The Royal Court and Stage Management wish to thank the following for their help with this production: Danial Morgenstern, LAMDA, The Old Suffolk Punch.

THE COMPANY

ANYA REISS (Writer)

FOR THE ROYAL COURT: Spur of the Moment.

AWARDS INCLUDE: TMA Best New Play for Spur of the Moment, Evening Standard Awards: Charles Wintour Award for Most Promising Playwright, Critics Circle Most Promising Playwright Award.

Anya was a member of Royal Court Young Writers' Programme in 2008. While on the Royal Court Studio Writers' group she wrote Spur of the Moment.

ELEANOR FOGG (Assistant Director)

AS DIRECTOR: One Day I Said No & So Lonesome I Could Cry (Desperate Men).

AS ASSISTANT DIRECTOR: Faith Healer (Bristol Old Vic).

AS ASSISTANT LINE PRODUCER: Swallows and Amazons (Bristol Old Vic).

PHOEBE FOX (Ruth)

THEATRE INCLUDES: As You Like It (Rose Theatre); A Month in the Country (Chichester Festival Theatre).

FILM: One Day.

SIMON GODWIN (Director)

FOR THE ROYAL COURT: Pagans (International Playwrights Season 2011), Wanderlust, Hung Over: Ten Short Plays About The Election (Rough Cut), Black Beast Sadness (Off the Wall Season Reading), Hassan Lekliche (I Come From There Season Reading).

OTHER THEATRE INCLUDES: Faith Healer, Far Away (Bristol Old Vic); The Winter's Tale (Headlong with Nuffield Theatre and Schtanhaus, UK tour); All the Little Things We Crushed (Almeida Projects); The Country (Tabard); The Seagull, Habeas Corpus, Relatively Speaking (Royal & Derngate Theatres, Northampton); Quartermaine's Terms (Royal & Derngate Theatres with Salisbury Playhouse); Mister Heracles (West Yorkshire Playhouse); Romeo & Juliet (Cambridge Arts Theatre); All's Well That Ends Well (Straydogs/UK Tour); Eurydice (Straydogs, BAC/Trafalgar Studios).

OPERA: Inkle and Yarico (Straydogs).

Co-founder of Straydogs Theatre Company.

Associate Director Royal & Derngate Theatres, Northampton (2001-2004).

Simon is currently an Associate Director of the Bristol Old Vic and the Royal Court.

VANESSA KIRBY (Dana)

THEATRE INCLUDES: As You Like It (West Yorkshire Playhouse); Women Beware Women (National); A Midsummer Night's Dream, Ghosts, All My Sons (Octagon Theatre, Bolton).

TELEVISION: The Hour.

AWARDS: Ian Charleson Award 2011 for A Midsummer Night's Dream, Women Beware Women and As You Like It, Ian Charleson Award Commendation 2010 for Ghosts, Biza Award for Emerging Talent at the Manchester Evening News Awards 2009.

DENIS LAWSON (Jim)

THEATRE INCLUDES: Le Cage Aux Folles (Playhouse Theatre, West End); Lust (Theatre Royal Haymarket/Walnut Street Theatre, Philadelphia); Oleanna (Duke of York's); Volpone (Almeida); The Importance of Being Earnest (Royalty Theatre); Ahes (Bush); Lend Me a Tenor (Shakespeare's Globe); Mr Cinders (King's Head/Fortune Theatre); Pal Joey (Albery); Bits of Lenny Bruce (King's Head).

TELEVISION INCLUDES: Hustle, Marchlands, Just William, Candy Cabs, Criminal Justice, Breaking the Mould, Enid Blyton's Super Adventure, No Holds Bard, Mumbai Calling, The Passion, Robin Hood, Jekyll, Dalziel and Pascoe, Bleak House, Sensitive Skin, Holby City, Lucky Jim, Fabulous Bagel Boys, Bob Martin, Other People's Children, The Ambassador, Royal Scandal, Natural Lies, Born Kicking, The Justice Game, One Way Out, Love After Lunch, The Uncertain Feeling, The Victoria Wood Show, The Kit Curran Radio Show.
FILM INCLUDES: Perfect Sense, Joyrider, Local Hero, The Chain, Providence, The Man in the Iron Mask.

NICK MANNING (Sound Designer)

FOR THE ROYAL COURT: The Empire (& Drum Theatre, Plymouth).

OTHER THEATRE INCLUDES: Twisted Tales (Lyric Hammersmith/Liverpool Playhouse/Northern Stage); Dick Whittington and His Cat, The Big Fellah (Out of Joint/Lyric Hammersmith); A Thousand Stars Explode in the Sky, Ghost Stories (Duke of York's, West End/Liverpool Playhouse/Lyric Hammersmith); Three Sisters, Jack and the Beanstalk, Comedians, The Jitterbug Blitz, Hang On, Cinderella, Spyski!, Depth Charge, Love – the Musical, The Birthday Party, The Resistible Rise of Arturo Ui, Beauty and the Beast, Accidental Heroes, Absolute Beginners, Ramayana, Metamorphosis, Too Close to Home, The Odyssey, Some Girls Are Bigger Than Others, The Firework-Maker's Daughter, Don Juan, Oliver Twist, Pericles, Camille, A Christmas Carol, The Prince of Homburg, Aladdin, The Servant, Pinocchio (Lyric Hammersmith); Gizmo Love, Excuses, Out of Our Heads (ATC); The Unsinkable Clerk (Network of Stuff); Grumpy Old Women 2, Britt on Britt, Grumpy Old Women (Avalon); Airsick, Crooked, When You Cure Me (Bush); Darwin in Malibu (Hampstead); The Master and Margarita (NYT); Rabbit (Frantic Assembly); Great Expectations(Bristol Old Vic).

Nick is Head of Sound at the Lyric Hammersmith.

MALCOLM RIPPETH (Lighting Designer)

FOR THE ROYAL COURT: Kin, Spur of the Moment.

OTHER THEATRE INCLUDES: The Umbrellas of Cherbourg (Kneehigh Theatre, West End); Brief Encounter (Kneehigh Theatre, West End/Broadway); Blast!, King of Prussia, Red Shoes, Don John, Cymbeline, Nights at the Circus, The Bacchae (Kneehigh Theatre); Six Characters in Search of an Author (Chichester/West End/UK & Australian tours); Calendar Girls (West End/Chichester/UK tour/Australia/Canada); The Field (Dublin); The Devil Inside Him (National Theatre Wales); The Winslow Boy, Dumb Show (Rose Kingston); Dark Side of Buffoon (Coventry/Lyric Hammersmith); His Dark Materials (Birmingham/Tour); Edward Gant's Amazing Feats of Loneliness, Faustus (Headlong Theatre); Crash, The Grouch, The Lion, The Witch and the Wardrobe, Homage to Catalonia (WYP); Mother Courage, Hamlet (ETT); James and the Giant Peach (Northampton); The Bloody Chamber, The Little Prince (Northern Stage); Trance (Bush); Confessions of a Justified Sinner, Copenhagen (Edinburgh Royal Lyceum); Monkey! (Dundee Rep); Tutti Frutti (National Theatre of Scotland).

OPERA & DANCE INCLUDES: Armida, Le Nozze Di Figaro, The Philosophers' Stone (Garsington); Carmen Jones (Royal Festival Hall); Seven Deadly Sins (WNO/Diversions Dance) and numerous productions for balletLORENT, most recently Designer Body and Blood, Sweat & Tears.

AWARDS INCLUDE: 2009 Theatregoers' Choice Award for Best Lighting Designer for Brief Encounter and Six Characters in Search of an Author and, as a member of the design team he won the 2010 OBIE Award for Brief Encounter in New York.

PAUL WILLS (Designer)

FOR THE ROYAL COURT: Breathing Corpses.

OTHER THEATRE INCLUDES: Novecento (Trafalgar Studios Donmar Season); Blasted (Lyric Hammersmith); Yerma (West Yorkshire Playhouse); The Stock Da'Wa (Hampstead Theatre Studio); A Number, Total Eclipse (Menier Chocolate Factory); Punk Rock (Lyric Hammersmith/Royal Exchange/tour); The Man Who Had All the Luck, The Cut (Donmar); Dandy in the Underworld, Overspill (Soho); Serious Money (Birmingham Rep); Nineteen Eighty-Four, Macbeth, See How They Run (Royal Exchange); Sisters, A Number, Gladiator Games, Blue/Orange (Sheffield Crucible); This Much Is True, Crestfall (Theatre503); House of Ghosts, Porridge (UK tour); Home (Theatre Royal Bath); The Frontline (Globe); I Ought to Be in Pictures (Manchester Library); Testing the Echo (Out of Joint, Tricycle); Pornography (Tricycle/Birmingham Rep/Traverse); Treasure Island (Kingston Rose); Mammals (Bush/Tour); Prometheus Bound (The Sound Venue, New York); The Field (Tricycle); The Changeling, Mother Courage (set, English Touring Theatre).

OPERA INCLUDES: Rusalka (English Touring Opera); Sweetness and Badness (Welsh National Opera); The Magic Flute (National Theatre of Palestine).

AWARDS: Paul's production of Blasted for the Lyric Hammersmith was the recipient of the 2011 Olivier Award for Outstanding Achievement in an Affiliate Theatre.

LYDIA WILSON (Jessica)

FOR THE ROYAL COURT: The Heretic.

OTHER THEATRE INCLUDES: Blasted (Lyric Hammersmith); Pains of Youth (National); The House of Special Purpose (Chichester Festival Theatre).

TELEVISION INCLUDES: South Riding, The Crimson Petal and the White, Any Human Heart, Pete Versus Life, Midsomer Murders.

FILM: Never Let Me Go.

JERWOOD
N E W P L A Y W R I G H T S

Since 1994 Jerwood New Playwrights has contributed to 68 new plays at the Royal Court including Joe Penhall's SOME VOICES, Mark Ravenhill's SHOPPING AND FUCKING (co-production with Out of Joint), Ayub Khan Din's EAST IS EAST (co-production with Tamasha), Martin McDonagh's THE BEAUTY QUEEN OF LEENANE (co-production with Druid Theatre Company), Conor McPherson's THE WEIR, Nick Grosso's REAL CLASSY AFFAIR, Sarah Kane's 4.48 PSYCHOSIS, Gary Mitchell's THE FORCE OF CHANGE, David Eldridge's UNDER THE BLUE SKY, David Harrower's PRESENCE, Simon Stephens' HERONS, Roy Williams' CLUBLAND, Leo Butler's REDUNDANT, Michael Wynne's THE PEOPLE ARE FRIENDLY, David Greig's OUTLYING ISLANDS, Zinnie Harris' NIGHTINGALE AND CHASE, Grae Cleugh's FUCKING GAMES, Rona Munro's IRON, Richard Bean's UNDER THE WHALEBACK, Ché Walker's FLESH WOUND, Roy Williams' FALLOUT, Mick Mahoney's FOOD CHAIN, Ayub Khan Din's NOTES ON FALLING LEAVES, Leo Butler's LUCKY DOG, Simon Stephens' COUNTRY MUSIC, Laura Wade's BREATHING CORPSES, Debbie Tucker Green's STONING MARY, David Eldridge's INCOMPLETE AND RANDOM ACTS OF KINDNESS, Gregory Burke's ON TOUR, Stella Feehily's O GO MY MAN, Simon Stephens' MOTORTOWN, Simon Farquhar's RAINBOW KISS, April de Angelis, Stella Feehily, Tanika Gupta, Chloe Moss and Laura Wade's CATCH, Mike Bartlett's MY CHILD, Polly Stenham's THAT FACE, Alexi Kaye Campbell's THE PRIDE, Fiona Evans' SCARBOROUGH, Levi David Addai's OXFORD STREET, Bola Agbaje's GONE TOO FAR!, Alia Bano's SHADES, Polly Stenham's TUSK TUSK and Tim Crouch's THE AUTHOR.

In 2010, Jerwood New Playwrights supported Bola Agbaje's OFF THE ENDZ, DC Moore's THE EMPIRE and Anya Reiss' SPUR OF THE MOMENT. Jerwood New Playwrights is supported by the Jerwood Charitable Foundation.

The Jerwood Charitable Foundation is dedicated to imaginative and responsible revenue funding of the arts, supporting artists to develop and grow at important stages in their careers. They work with artists across art forms, from dance and theatre to literature, music and the visual arts. www.jerwoodcharitablefoundation.org.

Anya Reiss's SPUR OF THE MOMENT
(photo: Keith Pattison)

Bola Agbaje's OFF THE ENDZ
(photo: Johan Persson)

THE ENGLISH STAGE COMPANY AT THE ROYAL COURT THEATRE

*'For me the theatre is really a religion or way of life.
You must decide what you feel the world is about
and what you want to say about it, so that everything
in the theatre you work in is saying the same thing
… A theatre must have a recognisable attitude. It will
have one, whether you like it or not.'*

George Devine, first artistic director of the
English Stage Company: notes for an unwritten
book.

photo: Stephen Cummiskey

As Britain's leading national company dedicated to new work, the Royal Court Theatre produces new plays of the highest quality, working with writers from all backgrounds, and asking questions about who we are and the world in which we live.

"The Royal Court has been at the centre of British cultural life for the past 50 years, an engine room for new writing and constantly transforming the theatrical culture." Stephen Daldry

Since its foundation in 1956, the Royal Court has presented premieres by almost every leading contemporary British playwright, from John Osborne's Look Back in Anger to Caryl Churchill's A Number and Tom Stoppard's Rock 'n' Roll. Just some of the other writers to have chosen the Royal Court to premiere their work include Edward Albee, John Arden, Richard Bean, Samuel Beckett, Edward Bond, Leo Butler, Jez Butterworth, Martin Crimp, Ariel Dorfman, Stella Feehily, Christopher Hampton, David Hare, Eugène Ionesco, Ann Jellicoe, Terry Johnson, Sarah Kane, David Mamet, Martin McDonagh, Conor McPherson, Joe Penhall, Lucy Prebble, Mark Ravenhill, Simon Stephens, Wole Soyinka, Polly Stenham, David Storey, Debbie Tucker Green, Arnold Wesker and Roy Williams.

"It is risky to miss a production there." Financial Times

In addition to its full-scale productions, the Royal Court also facilitates international work at a grass roots level, developing exchanges which bring young writers to Britain and sending British writers, actors and directors to work with artists around the world. The research and play development arm of the Royal Court Theatre, The Studio, finds the most exciting and diverse range of new voices in the UK. The Studio runs play-writing groups including the Young Writers Programme, Critical Mass for black, Asian and minority ethnic writers and the biennial Young Writers Festival. For further information, go to http://www.royalcourttheatre.com/playwriting.

"Yes, the Royal Court is on a roll. Yes, Dominic Cooke has just the genius and kick that this venue needs… It's fist-bitingly exciting." Independent

MAKING IT HAPPEN

The Royal Court develops and produces more new plays than any other national theatre in the UK. To produce such a broad and eclectic programme and all of our play development activities costs over £5 million every year. Just under half of this is met by principal funding from Arts Council England. The rest must be found from box office income, trading and financial support from private individuals, companies and charitable foundations. The Royal Court is a registered charity (231242) and grateful for every donation it receives towards its work.

You can support the theatre by joining one of its membership schemes or by making a donation towards the Writers Development Fund. The Fund underpins all of the work that the Royal Court undertakes with new and emerging playwrights across the globe, giving them the tools and opportunities to flourish.

MAJOR PARTNERSHIPS

The Royal Court is able to offer its unique playwriting and audience development programmes because of significant and longstanding partnerships with the organisations that support it.

Coutts & Co is the Principal Sponsor of the Royal Court. The Genesis Foundation supports the Royal Court's work with International Playwrights. Theatre Local is sponsored by Bloomberg. The Jerwood Charitable Foundation supports new plays by playwrights through the Jerwood New Playwrights series. The Artistic Director's Chair is supported by a lead grant from The Peter Jay Sharp Foundation, contributing to the activities of the Artistic Director's office. Over the past ten years the BBC has supported the Gerald Chapman Fund for directors.

The Harold Pinter Playwright's Award is given annually by his widow, Lady Antonia Fraser, to support a new commission at the Royal Court.

DEVELOPMENT ADVOCATES

Supported by
ARTS COUNCIL ENGLAND

PROGRAMME SUPPORTERS

PUBLIC FUNDING
Arts Council England, London
British Council
European Commission Representation in the UK

CHARITABLE DONATIONS
American Friends of the Royal Court
Martin Bowley Charitable Trust
The Brim Foundation*
Gerald Chapman Fund
City Bridge Trust
Cowley Charitable Trust
The H and G de Freitas Charitable Trust
The Edmond de Rothschild Foundation*
Do Well Foundation Ltd*
The Dorset Foundation
The John Ellerman Foundation
The Epstein Parton Foundation*
The Eranda Foundation
Genesis Foundation
J Paul Getty Jnr Charitable Trust
The Golden Bottle Trust
The Goldsmiths' Company
The Haberdashers' Company
Paul Hamlyn Foundation
Jerwood Charitable Foundation
Marina Kleinwort Charitable Trust
The Leathersellers' Company
Frederick Loewe Foundation*
John Lyon's Charity
The Andrew W Mellon Foundation
The Laura Pels* Foundation*
Jerome Robbins Foundation*
Rose Foundation
Royal Victoria Hall Foundation
The Peter Jay Sharp Foundation*
The Steel Charitable Trust
John Thaw Foundation
The Garfield Weston Foundation

CORPORATE SUPPORTERS & SPONSORS
BBC
Bloomberg
Coutts & Co
Ecosse Films
French Wines
Grey London
Kudos Film & Television
MAC

Moët & Chandon
Oakley Capital Limited
Sky Arts
Smythson of Bond Street

BUSINESS ASSOCIATES, MEMBERS & BENEFACTORS
Auerbach & Steele Opticians
Bank of America Merrill Lynch
Hugo Boss
Lazard
Louis Vuitton
Oberon Books
Savills
Vanity Fair

INDIVIDUAL MEMBERS

ICE-BREAKERS
Anonymous
Rosemary Alexander
Lisa & Andrew Barnett
Mrs Renate Blackwood
Ossi & Paul Burger
Mrs Helena Butler
Mr Claes Hesselgren & Mrs Jane Collins
Leigh & Lena Collins
Mark & Tobey Dichter
Ms P Dolphin
Elizabeth & James Downing
Virginia Finegold
Louisa Lane Fox
Charlotte & Nick Fraser
Alistair & Lynwen Gibbons
Mark & Rebecca Goldbart
Mr & Mrs Green
Sebastian & Rachel Grigg
Mrs Hattrell
Madeleine Hodgkin
Steven & Candice Hurwitz
Mrs R Jay
David Lanch
Yasmine Lever
Colette & Peter Levy
Mr & Mrs Peter Lord
David Marks QC
Nicola McFarland
Jonathan & Edward Mills
Ann Norman-Butler
Michael & Janet Orr
Mr & Mrs William Poeton
Really Useful Theatres
Mr & Mrs Tim Reid
Mrs Lois Sieff OBE
Nick & Louise Steidl
Torsten Thiele
Laura & Stephen Zimmerman

GROUND-BREAKERS
Anonymous
Moira Andreae
Simon Andrews
Nick Archdale
Charlotte Asprey
Jane Attias*
Caroline Baker
Brian Balfour-Oatts
Elizabeth & Adam Bandeen

Ray Barrell
Dr Kate Best
Dianne & Michael Bienes
Stan & Val Bond
Neil & Sarah Brener
Miss Deborah Brett
Sindy & Jonathan Caplan
Gavin & Lesley Casey
Sarah & Philippe Chappatte
Tim & Caroline Clark
Carole & Neville Conrad
Kay Ellen Consolver & John Storkerson
Clyde Cooper
Ian & Caroline Cormack
Mr & Mrs Cross
Andrew & Amanda Cryer
Alison Davies
Noel De Keyzer
Polly Devlin OBE
Rob & Cherry Dickins
Denise & Randolph Dumas
Zeina Durra & Saadi Soudavar
Robyn Durie
Glenn & Phyllida Earle
Allie Esiri
Margaret Exley CBE
Celeste & Peter Fenichel
Margy Fenwick
Tim Fosberry
The Edwin Fox Foundation
John Garfield
Beverley Gee
Mr & Mrs Georgiades
Nick & Julie Gould
Lord & Lady Grabiner
Richard & Marcia Grand*
Reade & Elizabeth Griffith
Don & Sue Guiney
Jill Hackel & Andrzej Zarzycki
Mary & Douglas Hampson
Sally Hampton
Sam & Caroline Haubold
Anoushka Healy
Mr & Mrs Johnny Hewett
Gordon Holmes
The David Hyman Charitable Trust
Mrs Madeleine Inkin
Nicholas Jones
Nicholas Josefowitz
Dr Evi Kaplanis
David P Kaskel & Christopher A Teano
Vincent & Amanda Keaveny
Peter & Maria Kellner*
Nicola Kerr
Philip & Joan Kingsley
Mr & Mrs Pawel Kisielewski
Maria Lam
Larry & Peggy Levy
Daisy & Richard Littler
James & Beatrice Lupton
Kathryn Ludlow
David & Elizabeth Miles

Barbara Minto
Ann & Gavin Neath CBE
Murray North
Clive & Annie Norton
Georgia Oetker
William Plapinger & Cassie Murray*
Andrea & Hilary Ponti
Wendy & Philip Press
Julie Ritter
Mark & Tricia Robinson
Paul & Gill Robinson
William & Hilary Russell
Julie & Bill Ryan
Sally & Anthony Salz
Bhags Sharma
Mrs Doris Sherwood
The Michael and Melanie Sherwood Charitable Foundation
Tom Siebens & Mimi Parsons
Richard Simpson
Anthony Simpson & Susan Boster
Samantha & Darren Smith
Brian Smith
Sandi Ulrich
The Ury Trust
Amanda Vail
Matthew & Sian Westerman
Mr & Mrs Nick Wheeler
Carol Woolton
Katherine & Michael Yates*

BOUNDARY-BREAKERS
Katie Bradford
Lydia & Manfred Gorvy
Ms Alex Joffe
Steve Kingshott
Emma Marsh
Paul & Jill Ruddock

MOVER-SHAKERS
Anonymous
Mr & Mrs Ayton
Cas Donald
Lloyd & Sarah Dorfman
Duncan Matthews QC
Ian & Carol Sellars
Edgar and Judith Wallner

HISTORY-MAKERS
Eric Abraham & Sigrid Rausing
Miles Morland

MAJOR DONORS
Rob & Siri Cope
Daniel & Joanna Friel
Jack & Linda Keenan*
Deborah & Stephen Marquardt
The David & Elaine Potter Foundation
Lady Sainsbury of Turville
NoraLee & Jon Sedmak*
Jan & Michael Topham
The Williams Charitable Trust

*Supporters of the AmericanFriends of the Royal Court (AFRCT)

FOR THE ROYAL COURT

Royal Court Theatre, Sloane Square, London SW1W 8AS
Tel: 020 7565 5050 Fax: 020 7565 5001
info@royalcourttheatre.com, www.royalcourttheatre.com

Artistic Director **Dominic Cooke**
Associate Directors **Simon Godwin, Jeremy Herrin*,
Sacha Wares***
Artistic Associate **Emily McLaughlin***
Diversity Associate **Ola Animashawun***
Education Associate **Lynne Gagliano***
Producer **Vanessa Stone***
Trainee Director **Monique Sterling‡**
PA to the Artistic Director **Pamela Wilson**

Literary Manager **Christopher Campbell**
Senior Reader **Nicola Wass****
Literary Assistant **Marcelo Dos Santos**
Studio Administrator **Clare McQuillan**
Writers' Tutor **Leo Butler***
Pearson Playwright **DC Moore ^**

Associate Director International **Elyse Dodgson**
International Projects Manager **Chris James**
International Assistant **William Drew**

Casting Director **Amy Ball**
Casting Assistant **Lotte Hines**

Head of Production **Paul Handley**
JTU Production Manager **Tariq Rifaat**
Production Administrator **Sarah Davies**
Head of Lighting **Matt Drury**
Lighting Deputy **Stephen Andrews**
Lighting Assistants **Katie Pitt, Jack Williams**
Lighting Board Operator **Jack Champion**
Head of Stage **Steven Stickler**
Stage Deputy **Dan Lockett**
Stage Chargehand **Lee Crimmen**
Chargehand Carpenter **Richard Martin**
Head of Sound **David McSeveney**
Sound Deputy **Alex Caplen**
Sound Operator **Sam Charleston**
Head of Costume **Iona Kenrick**
Costume Deputy **Jackie Orton**
Wardrobe Assistant **Pam Anson**

Executive Director **Kate Horton**
General Manager **Catherine Thornborrow**
Administrative Assistant **Holly Handel**

Head of Finance & Administration **Helen Perryer**
Senior Finance & Administration Officer
Martin Wheeler
Finance Officer **Rachel Harrison***
Finance & Administration Assistant **Tessa Rivers**

Acting Head of Marketing & Sales **Becky Wootton**
Acting Marketing Manager **Helen Slater**
Press & Public Relations Officer **Anna Evans**
Communications Assistant **Ruth Hawkins**
Communications Interns **Anoushka Arden,
Rhea Mehmet**
Sales Manager **Kevin West**
Box Office Sales Assistants **Stephen Laughton,
Helen Murray*, Ciara O'Toole, Amanda
Wilkin***

Head of Development **Gaby Styles**
Senior Development Manager **Hannah Clifford**
Development Manager **Lucy Buxton**
Development Officer **Penny Saward**
Development Assistant **Anna Clark**
Development Intern **Lucy Andrews**

Theatre Manager **Bobbie Stokes**
Duty Managers **Fiona Clift*, Elinor Keber***
Events Manager **Joanna Ostrom**
Bar & Food Manager **Sami Rifaat**
Bar & Food Assistant Managers **Ali Christian,
Becca Walton**
Head Chef **Charlie Brookman**
Sous Chef **Paulino Chuitcheu**
Bookshop Manager **Simon David**
Bookshop Assistant **Vanessa Hammick ***
Customer Service Assistant **Deirdre Lennon***
Stage Door/Reception **Simon David*, Paul
Lovegrove, Tyrone Lucas**

Thanks to all of our ushers and bar staff.

^This theatre has the support of the Pearson Playwrights' Scheme
sponsored by the Peggy Ramsay Foundation.

** The post of Senior Reader is supported by NoraLee & Jon
Sedmak through the American Friends of the Royal Court Theatre.

‡The post of the Trainee Director is supported by the BBC
writersroom.

* Part-time.

ENGLISH STAGE COMPANY

President
Dame Joan Plowright CBE

Honorary Council
**Sir Richard Eyre CBE
Alan Grieve CBE
Martin Paisner CBE**

Council
Chairman **Anthony Burton**
Vice Chairman **Graham Devlin CBE**

Members
**Jennette Arnold OBE
Judy Daish
Sir David Green KCMG
Joyce Hytner OBE
Stephen Jeffreys
Wasfi Kani OBE
Phyllida Lloyd CBE
James Midgley
Sophie Okonedo OBE
Alan Rickman
Anita Scott
Katharine Viner
Stewart Wood**

We've always been happy to be less famous than our clients

THE ACID TEST

Anya Reiss

THE ACID TEST

OBERON BOOKS
LONDON

WWW.OBERONBOOKS.COM

First published in 2011 by Oberon Books Ltd
521 Caledonian Road, London N7 9RH
Tel: +44 (0) 20 7607 3637 / Fax: +44 (0) 20 7607 3629
e-mail: info@oberonbooks.com
www.oberonbooks.com

A catalogue record for this book is available from the British
Library.

ISBN: 978-1-84943-045-6

Cover image by feastcreative.com

Printed in Great Britain by CPI Antony Rowe, Chippenham.

Characters

DANA LORRE, 22

RUTH JOHNSTON, 21

JESSICA BANK, 21

JIM BANK, 57

SETTING

A first-floor London flat's living room;

A sofa in the centre with an about-to-break coffee table in front overloaded with magazines, cups and an ashtray. A pile of cushions serve as a chair to the side and a small TV faces the sofa. Behind the sofa is another table with ipod speakers on it. There are girls' clothes and underwear drying on a clothes rack. The front door and a door to the kitchen are stage left while a corridor leading to the bedrooms and a door into the bathroom are stage right.

'In the real dark night of the soul it is always 3 o'clock in the morning, night after night'

F. Scott Fitzgerald

SCENE ONE

Friday 9pm. It's raining outside, in the empty flat you can hear running water, a clap of thunder then Laffy Taffy by D4L playing from the speakers. DANA LORRE emerges from the bedrooms wearing her bra and tracksuit bottoms. She dances around the room vaguely with a cigarette in her mouth and pours herself a glass of wine. She goes into the bathroom, the flat is empty again. She runs out with only a towel obviously having just got into the bath and disappears down the corridor, she returns with a razor and runs back into the bathroom and shuts the door. The doorbell rings, no response. It rings again and again. Someone starts bashing the door.

DANA: *(From the bathroom.)* I'm in the bath

GIRL'S VOICE: *(From outside the door.)* It's me! It's me!

DANA: I'm in the fucking bath

GIRL'S VOICE: Dana! It's me

DANA: I'm in the bath!

GIRL'S VOICE: Dana! It's me

DANA: I know it's you, I'm in the bath

GIRL'S VOICE: Dana?

DANA: Oh my fucking God!

RUTH JOHNSTON enters using her keys, a total mess and wet from the rain.

RUTH: Are you in the bath?

DANA: How did you get in?

RUTH: My key

DANA: Then why did you ring the door?

RUTH: I couldn't find it, I...I didn't want...can I come in?

DANA: No what the fuck is the matter with you?

RUTH: Dana Dana please

DANA: I'm in the bath

The handle turns.

DANA: Ruth! I'm naked; I'm in the bath, fuck off you fucking lesbian

RUTH: Get out then

DANA: Ruth you know the lock's broke. Don't come in

RUTH opens the door, eyes closed.

DANA: What the fuck Ruth? You are so fucking, fucking annoying you...pass me the towel

RUTH gropes on the floor, looking for the towel and throws it into the bathroom.

RUTH: Okay?

DANA: *(Comes out into the flat towel wrapped around her.)* What do you want?

RUTH: Can I have a bath?

DANA: What?

RUTH: Dana please I have had the worst fucking night of my life

DANA: What? Why? What's the matter with you? *(Turns the music off.)* You look angry

RUTH: I'm not angry! I'm upset!

DANA: Why?

RUTH: I don't want to talk about it

DANA: You just dragged me out the fucking bath

RUTH: Can you stop swearing at me?

DANA: Can you let me have a bath?

RUTH: Twix broke up with me

DANA: Oh shit

RUTH: Happy? Happy? You're so fucking...I'm so...*(Starts to cry.)*

DANA: Oh Ruth sorry, I didn't know, don't cry...umm...

DANA pulls the towel around her and gives RUTH a hug, RUTH wails, DANA is torn between sympathy and concern for her towel, RUTH pulls away.

RUTH: You're wet

DANA: So are you

RUTH: It's raining

DANA: Sit down

RUTH: I don't want to sit down

DANA: What do you want? You can have a bath

Ruth –You've used the hot water

DANA: Use my water

RUTH: But haven't you just started shaving?

DANA: Yeah well...

RUTH: That's disgusting

DANA: Well I didn't know you were gonna want the water did I?

RUTH: Well I didn't know we'd break up in the pouring rain did I?

DANA: Yeah I know I'm sorry

RUTH: I want a shower

DANA: We don't have...

RUTH: I know we don't have a shower

DANA: Sorry

RUTH: I want a drink

DANA: I can do that

RUTH: I want my fucking boyfriend

DANA: Let me get you a drink

RUTH starts crying lies down on the sofa DANA warily goes to the cupboard and brings out alcohol.

DANA: We have raspberry vodka

RUTH: *(Muffled.)* I don't care

DANA: And like another coloured thing, I can't read it, it's one of Imogen's Russian things she gave us

RUTH: I don't care

DANA: It looks really strong

RUTH: I don't care Dana I don't fucking care *(She starts hitting the sofa and screaming in anger.)*

DANA: Stop it

RUTH: I fucking don't care what the fuck type of vodka it is

DANA: Jesus *(Uncomfortable laugh.)* calm down

RUTH: *(Returning to crying again.)* I don't care

DANA: You are such a little psycho sometimes

DANA puts the drinks on the table, she watches RUTH cry hysterically for a second, looks to the bathroom.

DANA: I'm gonna put some clothes on okay? *(No reply.)* Okay?

DANA goes into the bathroom, you hear the water being let out, RUTH continues crying. She grows aware of DANA's absence and sits up, she sees the vodka. She unscrews and starts to drink it straight. DANA comes out as the noise of her crying has stopped.

DANA: Get a glass at least *(RUTH shakes her head.)* I'll get you a fucking glass

RUTH: I don't want a fucking glass

DANA runs and gets a glass and gives it to RUTH .

DANA: Two secs, pour me one too

DANA leaves and goes into the bathroom again. RUTH pours out shakily two drinks, she downs hers and has poured another by the time DANA comes out again, in her tracksuits and a floppy man's cardigan hair still wet, she passes RUTH a hoodie, she sits crossed legged next to RUTH on the sofa.

DANA: *(Taking a drink.)* Thanks *(RUTH looks at the floor about to cry, DANA looks at her.)* I'm sorry

RUTH: It's okay

DANA: Change

RUTH: Yeah… *(She takes her wet coat off and puts the hoodie on.)* thanks

DANA: Aw bubba *(She hugs RUTH who stays in the same position only allowing herself to be tipped towards DANA.)*

RUTH: I'm just so fucking angry

DANA: What happened?

RUTH: He broke up with me

DANA: Yeah but what happened?

RUTH: We had a fight and he broke up with me

DANA: What about?

RUTH: He was being such a fucking cunt and I was like what the fuck is wrong with you because he's been like that all week, I told you, he's been a fucking cunt all fucking week and he said 'oh it's because I'm depressed' and I was like fuck that. But I know he is really depressed and I've been trying to help him but he won't let me and I didn't want to piss him off in case…

DANA: Do you want a cigarette?

RUTH: Yeah

DANA gets up and starts to look for them.

RUTH: And I was like look I haven't been able to say anything in case you get angry at me and then you are depressed and I don't want to make it worse and I don't want you to do something stupid and he was like 'like what' and I said go back to doing fucking MDMA or something and then he was like 'you don't mean *that* much to me babe'

DANA: No

RUTH: Yeah and I was like what the fuck?

DANA: What a fucking cunt

RUTH: I know he is! He is such a fucking fucking cunt. Oh my god I'm so angry please can I have a cigarette

DANA: I'm looking for them

RUTH: Where's Jess?

DANA: Not back from her parent's yet

RUTH: Cigarette

DANA: Yeah I'm looking

RUTH: Please can I have one I'm like fucking freaking out give me a cigarette, give me a fucking cigarette

DANA: I can't find them

RUTH: Oh my god what the fuck *(She buries her head on the sofa and screams.)*

DANA: Okay don't go psycho

RUTH: Give me a fucking cigarette

DANA: *(Finds them.)* Here here, *(She lights it for RUTH.)* okay?

RUTH: Thank you

DANA: Jesus Christ *(Wandering off down the corridor she calls.)* So he broke up with you?

RUTH: Yeah kind of but I was really angry I mean I have never screamed that much in my life like people were looking at us so much I looked mental. Where have you gone?

DANA: *(Coming back with her phone.)* Where were you?

RUTH: On the bus

DANA: You were screaming at him on the bus?

RUTH: Yeah

DANA: *(Sits down and texts as she listens.)* Jesus

RUTH: I know and he was just like 'Ruth you are a fucking psycho go away' and so I did

DANA: And he let you?

RUTH: No he like chased me down the street because I like pushed the emergency stop on the bus so the doors opened, we were on Oxford Street

DANA: Fuck

RUTH: I know I like almost got run over and he was chasing after me like screaming 'what the fuck, where are you going I'll take you home'

DANA: How?

RUTH: I know that's what I said I was like how will you take me home? You don't have a fucking car do you? And in the end he like just threw like twenty quid at me and said get a fucking taxi and I said no

DANA: Why?

RUTH: I don't want his fucking money and he like threw it on the floor and he was like you fucking slut pick that up

DANA: He called you a slut?

RUTH: No but he was like pick that up

DANA: Oh

RUTH: And he like actually like threw me into a cab and told them to take me home and I was like crying all the way and the driver was like 'wow who was that guy?'

DANA: Shit

RUTH: And I was like my boyfriend and he said 'still darling'?

DANA: *(Cigarette in mouth.)* What the fuck the cab guy said that to you? *(She lights a cigarette.)*

RUTH: *(Not understanding her muffled voice.)* What?

DANA: The cab guy said that?

RUTH: What?

DANA: *(Taking the cigarette out her mouth.)* The cab guy said that to you?

RUTH: I know what the fuck I swear they can't say that

DANA: Do you want another drink?

RUTH: Yeah *(DANA pours herself a large one.)* and I was like going crazy in the cab I was like 'what the fuck' let me out let me out and he was like 'your fella told me to take you home' and I was like you are like holding me against my will this is like kidnap and stuff so he just pulled over like where Tesco's is

DANA: That's so far

RUTH: I know and I gave him all the money and had to like just walk back in the rain

DANA: Fucking hell. This is quite nice stuff

RUTH: Yeah it's really sweet

DANA: Has he called you?

RUTH: Yeah but I'm not picking up

DANA: Yeah he should have seen you home

RUTH: Yeah I know, I mean, *(She screams again.)* what the fuck?

DANA: Can you stop like screaming and shit it's scary

RUTH: Sorry, sorry just give me another drink?

DANA: Okay slow down

RUTH: No we're going to get fucked

DANA: Yeah but I got…

RUTH: Dana please

DANA: But I got stuff to do tomorrow

RUTH: Twix just broke up with me

DANA: I know

RUTH: So can you please get drunk with me? How often does my boyfriend break up with me?

DANA: Okay

RUTH: Promise

DANA: Yeah fine

RUTH: *(She lies on top of DANA, they both smoke.)* This has just been the worst day of my life

DANA: Yeah mine's been weird

RUTH: What happened to you? What's bad about your day?

DANA: No sorry talking about Twix

RUTH: What? Work?

DANA: No don't worry about it

RUTH: No go on

DANA: It doesn't matter leave it

RUTH: You can't just say that and not explain it

DANA: I didn't mean anything by it

RUTH: Why do I have to persuade you to tell me? You get in trouble at work?

DANA: No, they fucking love me

RUTH: Next Sir Alan

DANA: Exactly

RUTH: Wait he's not called that anymore

DANA: I'd so fuck Alan Sugar… too crude?

RUTH: A little, why?

DANA: I think he's amazing, but we wander off the point

RUTH: Which is?

DANA: Twix!

RUTH: No I don't want to talk about him

DANA: But my day isn't interesting

RUTH: Well talk about something else then

DANA: What?

RUTH: Talk about something else talk about something else…

DANA: Okay okay um…

RUTH: Dana talk about something else!

DANA: We need an anti-spider thing for the kitchen

RUTH: What?

DANA: I texted AQA about how to repel like spiders and you can make this thing

RUTH: What the fuck?

DANA: Like you need this like essence thing and they don't have it in Holland and Barrett even though I rung up first…

RUTH: We have spiders?

DANA: Yeah in the kitchen

RUTH: Ewww no please no why did you just tell me that?

DANA: You told me to talk about something else. Have another drink

RUTH: We have spiders!

DANA: Yeah like an infestation

RUTH: What! Oh my god how much worse can this day get?

DANA: Probably like a nest or something, do spiders have nests?

RUTH: Ew ew ew!

DANA: Like not a proper infestation

RUTH: Stop using that word

DANA: Infestation?

RUTH shivers and pours them both another drink.

DANA: We're overridden, overcome by an infestation, crawling in spiders

RUTH: Stop it

DANA: What?

RUTH: Just eurgh, vermin

DANA: Spiders aren't vermin

RUTH: Yeah they are

DANA: No like rats are vermin

RUTH: If there's too much of anything you call it vermin

DANA: …except humans

RUTH: You can call humans vermin

DANA: Yeah but then you're a Nazi

RUTH: Oh shit yeah

The two start to laugh, the drink is kicking in.

RUTH: Sorry for being a bitch, I'm going to be such bad company

DANA: Whatever, you seen my…

Both their phones go.

(In Borat's voice.) I have a text

They both look at their phones.

DANA: Terry

RUTH: Terry

DANA: *(Reading in a French accent.)* Come to Movida tonight, it looks like it's gonna be wild. Free drinks for all beautiful gals txt me for the guestlist, x, x, x

RUTH: *(French accent.)* Terry

DANA: *(French accent.)* Terry

RUTH: *(French accent and pointing at DANA.)* Terry

DANA: *(Does it back.)* Terry

RUTH: *(French accent still pointing.)* Terry and Dana sitting in a tree

DANA: Shut up

RUTH: *(Accent.)* doing terrible awful things they shouldn't be

DANA: *(Pushing her with a cushion.)* Shut up!

RUTH: *(Accent.)* in the bathrooms of Jalouse

DANA puts the cushion over her face, they struggle.

RUTH: He's not French apparently

DANA: Terry?

RUTH: Yeah apparently he comes from Essex, he thinks girls like French guys

DANA: Really?

RUTH: You did

DANA: Shut up! *(Tries to cushion her again.)*

RUTH: We should play 'I Never'

DANA: Fuck off

RUTH: Or Ring of Fire

DANA: With two of us?

RUTH: Yeah

DANA: You're drunk already

RUTH: Do like one of those eyeball shot things

DANA: I thought you were in the depths of despair

RUTH: Fuck off why did you remind me? You're such a fucking bitch

DANA: *(Taking her off.)* You're such a fucking bitch

RUTH: I can't believe he actually has…

DANA: Don't

RUTH: But…

DANA: *(Blocking her speaking.)* uh uh

RUTH: He…

DANA: Uh

RUTH: Dana…

DANA: Uh!

RUTH: *(Giving up and flopping back.)* Such a bitch

Pause.

RUTH: If you could go anywhere in the world where would you go?

DANA: Dunno

RUTH: I'd go to Japan

DANA: What! Why?

RUTH: Japanese people are funny

DANA: Oh yeah Japs are funny, from Hiroshima to Hello kitty its funny, funny, funny. *(RUTH laughs.)* And it's all like underwater now anyway *(RUTH opens her mouth in amused shock.)* What?

RUTH: *(Hitting her but laughing.)* Fine then I won't go

DANA: I'd go to India

RUTH: Why! You'd die

DANA: Er why?

RUTH: Like the water and the slums and shit and stuff

DANA: Yeah I know I've watched Slumdog Millionaire too! I know India's shit but I wouldn't stay in the slums I'd stay in a hotel

RUTH: Well that's like…wrong

DANA: Oh fuck off it be interesting

RUTH: *(Laughing.)* You so shouldn't say that

DANA: Why?

RUTH: *(Thinks about explaining but sighs.)* Can we play 'I Never' then?

DANA: But you know everything about me

RUTH holds up three fingers, DANA reluctantly does the same.

DANA: You go first

RUTH: I can't think of anything

DANA: You're the one that wants to play

RUTH: Start with anything

DANA: You start

RUTH: It can be boring

DANA: Can you just fucking start?

RUTH: Okay okay…I have never been to Disneyland

DANA: *(Drinking.)* That's boring *(Sees RUTH drink.)* you're meant to say something you've never done

RUTH: What?

DANA: That's the point to get other people drunk

RUTH: Oh

DANA: Okay so; I've never pushed the emergency stop on the bus and run off in Oxford Street

RUTH: Fuck off

DANA: Drink!

Suddenly a key turns in the door, JIM BANK and JESSICA BANK come through the door with bags and an umbrella

JESSICA: Hey guys, dad put your stuff in my room

JIM: Where's that?

JESSICA: Down the corridor second left

JIM: Okay but I thought, hello girls by the way, Ruth
sweetheart

RUTH: Hi Jim

JESSICA: Yeah sorry guys, down the corridor

JIM: I thought sofa

JESSICA: Yeah but put the rest of your junk in my room

JIM goes down the corridor, DANA and RUTH look bemused.

JESSICA: Sorry sorry had to bring him back

DANA: Er, who is that?

RUTH: Her dad

JESSICA: My dad

DANA: Oh

JESSICA: Sorry it's like *(Spots him coming back.)* like a fucking
nightmare

JIM returns, pyjamas in hand.

JIM: Need these

JESSICA: Um sorry dad, that's, that's *(Points out DANA.)* Dana

DANA: *(Raises her hand.)* Hello

JESSICA: This is my dad

JIM: *(Raises hand in an awkward wave.)* Jim

JESSICA: He's just going to stay a night or two

JIM: Sofa

JESSICA: Yeah on the sofa

JIM: Um if you don't mind

RUTH: Oh okay

JIM: If that's okay?

DANA: That's, that's fine with me *(To RUTH.)* I suppose

RUTH: And me

JIM: Good. Great.

JESSICA: Put that here for now

JIM: Ah yes okay *(Puts his pyjamas down carefully on the table behind the sofa.)*

RUTH: *(Mouthing quickly to JESSICA.)* What's going on?

JIM: Sorry. Should explain girls, um, bit of, bit of a spat back at, at, at HQ and um…

JESSICA: Him and mum had a bit of a fight

JIM: *(Laughs.)* Well just a bit

RUTH: I'm sorry

DANA: Yeah sorry

JESSICA: And I just said he should come down here for a bit to uh…clear

JIM: Clear my head

JESSICA: Yeah clear his head

JIM: Not that there's much clearing to do *(Attempts a laugh.)*

JESSICA: Only a couple of nights

JIM: Yes only a couple

JESSICA: I'm gonna get a spare duvet yeah?

JIM: Right you are

JESSICA leaves to the bedrooms.

JIM: Sorry Jessie said I could come down all a bit of a, a um well she said…

RUTH: No it's fine Jim

JIM: Thank you, just um sorry to crash the, what do you call it, oh the, the. Can't think, um help! Er, can't think of the word, that, that TV programme thing La-duh to lady

DANA: Ladette?

JIM: Yes yes ladette. *(DANA and RUTH smile.)* Sorry to crash the 'ladette' city pad

RUTH: No it's fine, haven't seen you for ages. Sit down *(Moves bottles from the sofa.)* wait

JIM: Sorry crashed some, some event here

RUTH: Oh no

JIM: Sorry

DANA: No we're not, this isn't a…

RUTH: We're not like this every night

JIM: Oh I'm sure

RUTH: No really

JIM: I won't tell your father

RUTH laughs.

JIM: How is he? Haven't seen him down the *(Does a little golf mime with a tongue click.)*

JESSICA returns.

JESSICA: Sit down dad

RUTH: Oh he's fine

JESSICA: Sit down

JIM: Right, 'kay. Feel a bit *(Sits on sofa between DANA and RUTH.)* feel a bit on show now

JIM grimaces to DANA and RUTH, they laugh.

JIM: So you're Dana right?

DANA: Yeah, hello

RUTH: *(Mouthing to Jessica.)* You okay?

JIM: Funny to meet you now

JESSICA shrugs to RUTH.

DANA: I know

JIM: I've seen a photo

DANA: Oh yeah

JIM: Oh well, no, not like…

DANA: I didn't think…

JIM: No well you would…of the, of the flat when the two of you just moved in

DANA: Oh yeah I remember that

JIM: Ages ago

DANA: Yeah like, what was that Jess?

JESSICA: Second year

DANA: Yeah so what's that?

JESSICA: Two

DANA: Yeah two years ago

JIM: It was you and Jessie with all these boxes still about and that, that other girl what was her name? The pretty girl who went to UCL with you?

JESSICA: Kim

ANYA REISS

DANA: Yeah Kim

JIM: And she, she went, she left didn't she, she um…

JESSICA: Australia

JIM: Oh! Really? She's on holiday

DANA: No she moved back her family were Australian

JIM: Really? She didn't look Australian

JESSICA: She didn't look Australian?

JIM: Well no

JESSICA: *(Walking out.)* Cause they all usually wear cork hats, are sunburnt and have barbeque spits for hands

JIM hasn't taken all of his stuff so JESSICA picks some up and leaves to put it in her bedroom.

JIM: *(Calling after her.)* Oh yes okay, alright, alright very droll *(To DANA and RUTH.)* She's not too happy with me

RUTH: Why not?

JIM: God knows, probably takes after her mother

They laugh as JESSICA comes back in.

JIM: It *is* a nice flat isn't it?

RUTH: Love it

JIM: Not keeping it that tidy though are you?

RUTH: No it is usually

DANA: It's quite like fucked up *(RUTH gives her a look.)* …sorry

JIM: What?

DANA: I'm a bit drunk I don't swear all the time

JIM: Oh no, God no don't worry about me. Old enough to just about handle the odd clanger

RUTH: Do you want a drink Jim?

JIM: Oh well

DANA: Yeah go on Jim, make him one Ruth

JIM: Oh a small one

RUTH: So a big one *(Gives JIM the drink.)*

JIM: *(Laughs.)* So this is where my money goes Jessie?

JESSICA: Your money?

RUTH: You don't still give her money do you?

JIM: Course

JESSICA: A bit here and there

RUTH: *(To JESSICA.)* You liar

JESSICA: A few hundred now and then is not the same…

DANA: She always goes on about it being 'all her savings'

JIM: Oh well it is a bit

JESSICA: A bit!

JIM: Well Jessie a lot of that did come from my mother when she died

JESSICA: Dad

JIM: What?

JESSICA: *(To him, privately.)* Stop it

JIM: *(Hands up.)* Oh alright alright

JESSICA: She was my grandma and she died and left me money

JIM: Okay okay

JESSICA: Sorry if you are a little bit further up the family tree tha…

JIM: Calm down, calm down darling *(He laughs.)* Ok? *(JESSICA makes a non-committal type of nod and JIM turns back to DANA and RUTH.)* Jesus Christ this is very strong thought I was being a wimp but really

JESSICA: Guys make him a normal one

JIM: No it's fine, fine

DANA: Single life means double shots *(DANA laughs to herself slightly drunkenly, RUTH hits her.)* Ow

JIM: No no don't worry

JESSICA: It'll all blow over don't worry

JIM: No well

JESSICA: It will dad

RUTH: Yeah everyone has big fights sometimes

DANA: Yeah my parents all the time before they got divorced

JIM: Oh well er…

DANA: Sorry not that you…

RUTH: Anyway it was just a fight

JIM: Well…

RUTH: Wasn't it?

DANA: *(To JESSICA.)* Was just a fight right?

JESSICA: Guys leave it

JIM: No well it's fine girls don't worry about it

RUTH: You'll make up

JIM: Well um…

DANA: Like what happened?

RUTH and DANA look fascinated, JIM is unsure of what to say.

JESSICA: Give him a break

JIM: Well um I suppose if I'm going to be kipping here probably should just say

RUTH: You don't have to

DANA: Yeah you don't like have to

JIM: You are both sweet but well Fiona…

DANA: *(Checking with JESSICA.)* Your mum?

JESSICA: Yeah

JIM: Yes her mum, my wife etcetera um, well I have been removed from the house…surgically

JESSICA: Dad you don't…

JIM: Translated as thrown out. I've been thrown out

RUTH: Your mum threw him out?

JESSICA: Kind of

RUTH: Kind of?

JIM: No well not really a kind of, possibly thing pretty much um…out. All rather terrifying actually she can be a bit, *(To RUTH.)* well you know all rather, argh *(He makes a little claw face.)*

JESSICA: Dad

JIM: Ever wonder where she got it from? *(Looks to her.)* Sorry am I being an embarrassment?

JESSICA: *(Trying to laugh in front of RUTH and DANA.)* Dad fucking hell

JIM: Okay okay, zip. No I'm a homeless man, James Bank is officially homeless! And my good old daughter took me in to keep me from Woolworths' gutter

DANA: Not Woolworths anymore

JIM: Oh yes that's right. Even my gutter has been taken from me. You know what Dana *(Passing his glass over.)* really wouldn't mind another

RUTH: And so would I

DANA: Jess?

RUTH: Yeah come on stop being boring and have a drink

JESSICA: Fine

DANA: Yeah?

JESSICA: Yeah

JESSICA comes forward and takes a drink.

JESSICA: *(To JIM about his drink.)* You alright with that?

JIM: Cheers

JIM tries to clink glasses with his daughter, she looks angry again.

RUTH: Thank you

DANA: Right

They all have their drinks.

JIM: Okay. Let's drink our troubles away

SCENE TWO

11pm, same night. DANA and RUTH sit either side of JIM, JESSICA is on the cushion chair. They have been drinking all this time.

DANA: You know Ben, my boss, Ben Tevers

RUTH: The ginger guy

DANA: Yeah but he's quite like…he's not ginger in like a Rupert Grint-y way he is a hot ginger

JESSICA: Don't exist

DANA: Yeah they do like Sean Slater from Eastenders and, and that guy that does the army and shouty stuff like Damien Lewet

JESSICA: Lewis

DANA: What?

JESSICA: Damien Lewis

DANA: Yeah he's hot

JESSICA: He's hot despite being ginger like a disability he's overcome

JIM: I looked a bit ginger when I was younger

JESSICA: No you didn't

JIM: In certain lights, probably looked a bit like this Damien Lewit

JESSICA: *(DANA laughs.)* Lewis, you just heard me say that

RUTH: Get on with it

DANA: What?

RUTH: What about Ben?

DANA: Like he… you don't mind do you Jim?

JIM: Sorry?

DANA: I mean you don't mind me saying

JIM: I don't know what you're going to say do I?

JESSICA: Ben…

JIM: Don't rush her

DANA: No well Ben…I asked Ben to take me to that dinner you know the one at the Savoy

RUTH: With the contract guy?

DANA: Yeah *(For JIM's benefit.)* like there is this big dinner with everyone from work and the sister company which actually makes more money and they are looking for people to transfer so I want to go and I said to Ben would he take me

JIM: Okay you shrewd business networker

DANA: Yeah well like yeah. And he, Ben, my boss was all like 'so you're asking me out' and I was like, I was like kind of 'not really Mr Tevers' because I don't know I was being a bit flirty and stuff

RUTH: Standard

DANA: And I don't know what to do

JIM: Sorry what's the problem?

DANA: It's like he'll take me and stuff

JIM: Good

DANA: Yeah but like you know

JIM: God you girls say 'like' a lot, what does like mean

DANA: Sorry it's like... fuck, it's lik...its a nervous thing

JIM: It's a grammar thing

JESSICA: Dana what's the problem?

DANA: What?

JESSICA: Will he not take you?

DANA: No he said he would if like, shit sorry, if, he might you know if like...

She and JIM laugh.

JESSICA: What?

DANA: You know go out with him

JIM: I thought you had to go out with him to the dinner

DANA: No like, like…

JESSICA: Can you just say it?

DANA: Oh it doesn't matter

RUTH: Oh not this again

DANA: No it doesn't matter

RUTH: Not begging to know are we Jess

JESSICA: Nope

DANA: Yeah it doesn't matter

JIM: No go on sweetheart go on

RUTH: No leave it Jim we're not going to be all 'oh go on tell us Dana please'

JESSICA: 'So desperate to know'

RUTH: 'You must, must tell us'

DANA: No I won't it's embarrassing talk about something else

JIM: No Dana go on you've caught my interest

DANA: No it's nothing just Ben you know

JESSICA: No we don't know

DANA: Like he will take me and everything it's just… you know

RUTH: No what?

DANA: *(Hiding her face and saying it really quickly.)* If I have sex with him

JESSICA: *(Couldn't hear.)* What?

DANA: *(Still hiding her face.)* If I have sex with him

RUTH: What?

DANA: *(Eyes shut.)* If. I. Have. Sex. With. Him

RUTH: Wow what?

DANA dives face down in the sofa embarrassed, RUTH and JESSICA pull at her a bit amused.

JESSICA: If you what?

RUTH: Fucking hell

DANA: *(Face still in the sofa.)* No no it doesn't matter

JESSICA: Sit up

DANA: No it doesn't matter

RUTH: Fucking report him

DANA: No you don't understand and I want to go to this dinner

JESSICA: *(Laughs.)* They've just done up the Savoy

DANA: Yeah I know, I looked on the website it looks amazing

RUTH: Have you both gone fucking mad?

DANA: No you don't understand I like him and he wasn't like 'you must have sex with me'

JESSICA: What was he like?

DANA: Like you know like 'oh so if you're going to be my date it better be a proper date' and stuff

JESSICA: Are you sure he meant you have to have sex he wasn't just flirting

DANA: No like at first but then he was obviously so serious because he said 'I want to see you before we go then, check we are compatible'. And he was saying he isn't doing anything tonight and...

RUTH: What a fucking creep

DANA: No he's like really sexy and wasn't doing it in a creepy way

RUTH: He's a freak

DANA: Shut up you don't understand, like Jess what do you think?

JESSICA: I dunno like…

JIM: It doesn't sound very Kosher does it

JESSICA: Kosher? What are you a fucking East End diamond dealer?

RUTH: You watch Snatch way to much Jess

JIM: God you lot are fascinating

DANA: What shall I do?

JIM: Well as a young man about town…

RUTH and DANA laugh.

JESSICA: Young?

JIM: Young for a man to have children your age. Well maybe not nowadays girls but to us, in my day was quite young not like all these kids nowadays with kids. I mean your mother didn't lose her virginity until she was 19…

JESSICA: Stop!

JIM: and she was perfectly normal

RUTH: *(Teasing.)* Knew Jess took after someone

JESSICA: Ruth fuck's sake

JIM: What? What's this?

JESSICA: It doesn't matter

JIM: Did you only lose your virginity when you were 19, no I don't believe that you went out with that little fat boy when you were 16. Me and your mother always thought you had made love to…

JESSICA: Dad…

JIM: Oh sex, fine whatever you all call it. We used to say shag, am I hideously out of date?

JESSICA: Dad you are really drunk do you want to go to bed

JIM: Jessica Maria Rosemary Bank are you trying to put your own father to bed?

JESSICA: Dad you are so. Fucking. Drunk

RUTH: He's not that drunk Jess

JIM: Exactly

RUTH: Leave him be

JIM: Nicely tinted, tinged with drunkenness

DANA: Same

JESSICA: Dad, you can sleep in my room, go to bed

JIM: No you go to bed I am perfectly happy where I am

JESSICA: Fuck's sake

JIM: Where was I girls?

RUTH: *(Giggling.)* You were talking about 'shagging'

JIM: Oh well got to learn all that stuff all over again, god what an effort was bad enough the first time. What's it that mum says in Friends?

RUTH: You watch Friends?

JIM: Was on day and night in our house, when the mousy one's mother is um talking to her daughter about…

DANA: Oh, oh I know what you're talking about. 'So tell me what's new in sex'

JIM: Yes! *(DANA and RUTH laugh.)* Am I being like that?

JESSICA: Yes so shut the fuck up

DANA: Oh my god you're so mean!

JIM: Ah she always picks on me girls

DANA: Don't worry Jim we'll protect you!

RUTH: We're on Jim watch

The girls kneel either side of JIM and hold their drinks and cigarettes up forming a cross above his head.

JIM: Well aren't I the lucky one? Surrounded by two gorgeous barely clothed drunk women...and my daughter

RUTH: Gorgeous?

DANA: Are we really gorgeous Jim?

JIM: And you both know it

DANA laughs and falls from her position.

JESSICA: Oh my god

RUTH: Dana when I was little I'd come round to Jess's house and she'd be so mean to her dad...

JIM: Ah what's changed?

JESSICA: Oh for fuck's sake

JESSICA gets up and goes to her room.

RUTH: Dana, Dana she'd be so mean and her mum was always mean to him and I always just wanted to see him happy. He, you Jim, you always looked so sad

JIM: I'm a downtrodden man

RUTH: But now we've both been cut free

JIM: Hm?

DANA: She broke up with her boyfriend tonight but he was a cunt

RUTH: No he wasn't

DANA: He was all arty and skinny and 'troubled'

RUTH: Shut up

JIM: But that's Ruth's type isn't it always knew you'd have someone like that

RUTH: See Jim's really, really int, intuit-ti-tive

JIM: Am I?

RUTH: Yes *(Leans on JIM.)*

JIM: *(To DANA.)* Had a bit too much to drink this one

DANA: We all have

JIM: That's true

DANA: Another?

JIM: Please

JIM is trapped by RUTH so DANA makes them another drink.

RUTH: Can you tell what type Dana would like?

JIM: Oh well I've known you much longer

RUTH: Try

DANA: Yeah try

JIM: A much more straight-talking kind

DANA: Yeah…

JIM: And um…tall?

JESSICA comes out of her room and listens, unseen.

DANA: Well…

JIM: Quite tall, like six two. Quite muscly

DANA: *(Laughing, as is RUTH, both seem to think he has a gift.)* Yeah

JIM: Clever, not too book smart or anything but just really intelligent and witty

RUTH: Oh my god this is so him

DANA: Go on

JIM: You probably wouldn't mind if he was a little older than you because you want him to be successful. Pretty flirty. Am I right?

DANA: Yeah you're right

JESSICA: And ginger

DANA: Oh fuck off Jess

RUTH: Jim you are so right you just described her perfect man

JESSICA: Or any 21 year old girl's perfect man

RUTH: Not mine

JESSICA: Any normal 21 year old girl then

JESSICA disappears into the bathroom.

DANA: Ignore her she's such a kill joy sometimes

RUTH: What would *(She lowers her voice and points.)* she like?

They all lower their voices becomes quite pantomimey with lots of actions.

JIM: *(Mouthing and pointing to the bathroom.)* Jessie?

DANA nods and pats him encouraging him to guess.

JIM: *(Shrugging.)* I dunno

RUTH: Try

JIM: *(Shrugs again.)* I dunno. Does she…does she like men?

DANA and RUTH delighted open mouthed, DANA starts laughing.

RUTH: Oh my God

JIM: Does she?

RUTH: Oh my God Dana

The two laugh together, JIM grins.

JIM: Does she?

RUTH: *(Nodding but still laughing.)* Yes, yes

DANA: We don't know for sure though do we

RUTH: *(Hits DANA but they laugh more.)* Shut up

JIM: Oh God is she still…

> *JESSICA comes out of the bathroom, they all try to stop laughing. She rolls her eyes and goes back to the bedrooms, they start laughing again really badly.*

DANA: Oh my god, oh my god, oh my god

RUTH: Did she hear us?

JIM: No, no is she a…is she still a…you know

DANA: What?

JIM: A virgin?

> *DANA and RUTH look at each other bite their lips. RUTH nods.*

JIM: Oh

DANA: Oh my god just change the conversation

JIM: Yes we should

RUTH: How did we even get onto this?

DANA: Twix

JIM: What?

RUTH: Oh yeah. No my boyfriend

JIM: Didn't you just say Twix?

RUTH: That's his name

JIM: Oh dear

DANA laughs.

RUTH: No well it's not his real name but everyone calls him
Twix

JIM: Why on earth do they do that?

RUTH: He's called Johnny Twixern, Twix?

JIM: It's his second name?

RUTH: Yeah

DANA: I know how tragic is that? It's so fucking public school

RUTH: Oh shut up

JIM: What and you've broken up with this er, Twix?

RUTH: Yeah today, actually can we not...you know

JIM: No I totally understand

RUTH: Just feels really like...

JIM: No, no same boat here don't worry about it

DANA: We should get Jess back out here?

RUTH: She's in a mood

DANA: Don't worry about it, we'll just make her drink some
more

RUTH: But you drank all her vodka

DANA: *(Calling.)* Jess

RUTH: *(To JIM.)* Out of spite not necessity

JIM laughs, JESSICA comes out.

JESSICA: What?

DANA: Stop being such a fucking moody bitch come sit down

JESSICA: I'm working

RUTH: If me and Jim who've both had our hearts broken today can stay to party so can you

JESSICA: Why have you had your heart broken?

DANA: She broke up with Twix

JESSICA: What?

DANA: Don't don't don't, we are not talking about it sit down

JESSICA: Fine whatever

JESSICA takes out her cigarettes.

JIM: Jessie!

JESSICA: What you're going to be my father now?

JIM: You smoke?

JESSICA: Yes

JIM: Good god daughter's turned into Amy Winehouse and no one told me

RUTH: Do you like Amy Winehouse?

JESSICA: You going to stay here you have to shut up about me smoking *(She lights her cigarette.)*

RUTH: You touched a nerve

JIM: Apparently

RUTH: She hates the fact that she smokes

DANA: She's afraid of dying, I however look death and my own mortality straight in the eye and say come and get me *(Takes JESSICA's cigarette, she puts her hand down to stop her.)* You owe me

JESSICA: And you owe me a fiver

DANA: I don't have any cash

JESSICA: Then you don't have any of my cigarettes

DANA: I have some I just can't be bothered to find them

JESSICA: You are going to have to find them or find the money

DANA: Okay, okay look *(She produces lighters from various places.)* There, there are five lighters that's worth five pounds give me a cigarette

JESSICA: You said you'd pay me five pounds back not goods up to the value of

DANA: Don't be a freak

JESSICA: I don't need five lighters

DANA: Yeah you do Jess, can you just grow up and give me a fucking cigarette?

RUTH: And me

DANA: And Ruth

JESSICA: Fine fine *(She opens the pack offers DANA and RUTH who take one, she offers JIM defiantly, he shakes his head.)*

RUTH: I'm really hungry

DANA: So am I

JIM: Shall I make us something, earn my keep?

RUTH: Oh no Jim you don't have to do that

JESSICA: We don't have any chicken

DANA: What?

JESSICA: Dad can only cook chicken

JIM: Now that's not true…I can fry chicken, I can roast chicken, I can grill chicken, I can sauté chicken, I can boil chicken, damn it I can even burn chicken too

RUTH: I forgot about this

JIM: I'm a real modern man

RUTH: I'm a vegetarian nowadays though Jim so don't worry

JIM: There's a surprise

RUTH playfully slaps him.

DANA: Did you grow up on a chicken farm or something?

JIM: No because then I'd be good at eggs too wouldn't I? I don't know how it happened but it is truly, the only thing I can cook. God bestowed on me one gift in the kitchen he saw me and said Jim Bank I give thee chicken and I looked up to God and I said thank you God I am most fond of this feathered bird especially when stripped of its feathers is there another gift perhaps? And he…

JESSICA: Well we don't want it

RUTH: No go on

JIM: What?

JESSICA: No don't get him started. We've got crisps and stuff

JIM: Righto

DANA: Look in the top cupboards okay?

JESSICA: If you can manage that

JIM: Stop it *(He points at her, standing rather close to where she is sitting.)*

JESSICA: Stop what?

JIM: *(Very firmly, almost like to a dog.)* Just stop it

JESSICA: Don't be pathetic

JIM: I'm not the one being pathetic

JESSICA: Can you just go and get the crisps or something

JIM: You are embarrassing yourself

JESSICA: Can you go *(She tries to push his hand away from her face but he grabs that hand and stops her.)*

JIM: I'm warning you. Stop it

JESSICA: Fine

JIM: *(Turning away from JESSICA.)* Right crisps and stuff, top
cupboard, kitchen

JIM goes to the kitchen.

JESSICA: I'm sorry about my dad

DANA: No he's cool

RUTH: I love your dad

JESSICA: He's being fucking annoying I'm really sorry

DANA: No it's cool I like him he's funny

JESSICA: I had to bring him back he was all *(Gestures 'messed
up'.)*

RUTH: I can't believe your mum kicked him out

JESSICA: Well she like, not really

RUTH: Poor Jim

DANA: Yeah be a bit nicer to him Jess

JESSICA: What?

RUTH: You're being such a bitch to him

JESSICA: What?

DANA: You are a bit

JESSICA: You don't know what he's like

RUTH: Oh sorry does he beat you every night with a
broomstick?

JESSICA: Oh fucking typical, must be my fault.

RUTH: You're being a bitch

JESSICA: Just because he's a little lost looking and pathetic must be my fault, you such a sucker Ruth 'aw bless look at the big overgrown baby'

DANA: Oi chill out Jess, you alright?

JESSICA: What?

DANA: Your mum and everything

JESSICA: Yeah whatever

RUTH: Just think if it's hard for you it's harder for him

JESSICA: Why do you always take the guy's side, you don't even know him

RUTH: He's hardly a stranger

JESSICA: And you know that I'm a heartless bitch?

DANA: *(Smiling.)* Kind of Jess

JESSICA: Fuck off

RUTH: What's your dad ever done to you?

JESSICA: Nothing

RUTH: So why do you hate him?

JESSICA: I don't hate him

DANA: Oh whatever guys...

RUTH: Why are you so mean to him?

JESSICA: Why's he so mean to me?

RUTH: Because you're being mean to him

JESSICA: What I started it? It's always been me since the beginning maybe I threw up on him when I was baby and that's what started it?

DANA: What, he was mean to you when you were younger?

JESSICA: Kind of

RUTH: Bullshit he always came to the school plays and picked you up and everything, I was there and I remember

JESSICA: Yeah falling asleep in the plays and coming late and not remembering my year or friends or anything

RUTH: You can't seriously hate him for that! That's just standard dad stuff Jess you haven't suffered particularly

JESSICA: Okay sorry I wasn't abused, sorry my dad didn't fuck me

DANA: *(Protesting to the crudeness.)* Oh Jess!

JESSICA: Sorry he didn't cheat on my mum and beat her, I'm sorry he didn't kill my dog

RUTH: What the fuck?

JESSICA: What? Can't I just be fed up of him this mild mannered thing. This fucking *(Struggling for the right words.)* vanilla, fucking natural yoghurt following me round

DANA bursts out laughing.

RUTH: Oh it must be so hard for you Jess

JESSICA: What? What cause there are kids raped in Africa I can't hate my dad or something *(DANA laughs again.)* that's not the point.

RUTH: Then what is the point? Can you stop fucking laughing Dana

JESSICA: The point is you are having a go at me for being like that with my dad but my relationship doesn't have to be fucking measured to the extremity of cruelty for me to not be totally happy with everything

RUTH: I don't even know what you're saying anymore

JESSICA: Okay put simply…

RUTH: Don't be fucking patronising

JESSICA: I'm not being patronising I'm saying put simply because you didn't understand…

RUTH: It's not not understanding you weren't making any sense

JESSICA: No you just don't understand what I was saying

RUTH: Okay yeah sorry I don't have a fucking degree in being a fucking high-minded bitch

JESSICA: That's why I said put simply

RUTH: You can just rephrase it instead of being patronising

JESSICA: That's what I'm trying to fucking do

RUTH: Then go on then I'm listening

JESSICA: You can't say my feelings don't count because my dad wasn't a smack head or something

DANA: Aw poor Jim

RUTH: He hasn't done anything wrong

JESSICA: Exactly. I dunno what to do with him, I want more from him. I want less even

There's a crash in the kitchen and from off you can hear:

JIM: Bugger

JESSICA: *(Calling to JIM.)* What the fuck are you doing?

JIM: Getting crisps and stuff, everything's under control

JESSICA: You're taking ages

JIM: Can you leave me to it Jess?

JESSICA: Don't call mum

JIM: I'm not

JESSICA: I'm trying to help you

JIM: Don't tell me what to do

JESSICA walks away from the kitchen back to the sofa.

JESSICA: Fucking hell he's being an idiot

RUTH: Leave him alone!

JESSICA: I'm allowed to feel how I want about my own dad and treat him how I want when he is in my flat

RUTH: Our flat and you are making it fucking shit for the rest of us, just leave him be

JESSICA: Sorry *(sits down.)* girls are always there for each other, so glad I'm here with my understanding friends who are so sympathetic towards my feelings

DANA: Your feelings don't count because you're drunk

RUTH: I just broke up with Twix

JESSICA: What a fucking tragedy

DANA: Oh fuck's sake shut up you two Jesus you both are so like highly strung, like I dunno just calm down we can order some Chinese or like just have another drink

JESSICA: Ah that's always the answer

DANA: Do you want to piss everyone off?

JIM emerges for a second.

JIM: I am making a feast, you have strawberries and dark chocolate

DANA: Do we?

RUTH: That was going to be for me and Twix

JIM: Oh I'm so sorry

RUTH: No no forget it shall we have it now?

JIM: Exactly what I was going to ask

DANA: Yeah

JIM: Dark chocolate and strawberries powerful aphrodisiacs

JIM disappears into the kitchen and DANA and RUTH laugh.

JESSICA: Eurgh he is so…cringe. *(About them laughing.)* And you're both so drunk

DANA: Oh bubba, bubba *(DANA gets up, grabs a drink and sits on JESSICA's lap.)* Can you please cheer up

JESSICA: Get off

DANA: *(In a baby voice.)* You look so miserable

JESSICA: Stop

DANA: *(Still in voice.)* You're in a big grumpy grump

JESSICA: Why are you doing a Chinese accent?

DANA: *(Still in voice.)* I'm not doing a Chinese accent this is my cute accent to make you stop being such a moody fucking cow to everyone and I can see it is working

JESSICA: *(Laughing.)* Get the fuck off me

DANA: *(Still in voice.)* Then we are going to have to go to plan b

JESSICA: What?

DANA: Drink up *(She holds the drink to her mouth, JESSICA plays along.)* and all the way *(JESSICA downs it.)*

JESSICA: Fuck me that was so strong

DANA: Good and now you will have caught up

JESSICA: Yeah?

DANA: Yeah. You two friends?

JESSICA: I was only trying to make a point

DANA: Guys

RUTH: It's cool, we're cool

JESSICA: *(Winking.)* That's right darling

RUTH: Yes darling

DANA: Right. Let's play Dares

JESSICA: Yeah

DANA: See one drink and she livens right up!

RUTH: I dare you two to kiss

DANA: Oh boring

RUTH's phone rings.

JESSICA: You're so un-fucking original Ruth

RUTH cancels the call.

DANA: Twix?

RUTH: *(Half nods.)* Are you going to do it then?

DANA: Fine, come here sweetheart

DANA and JESSICA kiss.

RUTH: *(As they are kissing.)* I should call your dad out here

DANA snorts into laughter mid-kiss and has to pull away she and RUTH are in hysterics, JESSICA is smiling.

JESSICA: Shut up

DANA: *(Hitting JESSICA.)* No no you don't understand

JESSICA: What?

RUTH: He thought, Jim thought…

DANA: He asked if you were a lesbo

JESSICA: What?

DANA: He was like 'she does like men right?'

JESSICA: He said that?

RUTH: I swear I almost pissed myself

JESSICA: *(Trying to get up.)* Oh my god he is such a fucking bastard

DANA: *(Stops her from getting up.)* Stop it don't start that again, please can the fun Jess please come out and stay?

JESSICA: He's such a fucking bastard, he knows I'm not, he's just trying to embarrass…

RUTH: You are being paranoid! He didn't know that you hadn't slept with Jack and now he doesn't know what to think

JESSICA: Shut up I'm not a fucking lesbian and he knows that

RUTH: Yeah but you are 21 and a virgin and that's like pretty unusual so…

JESSICA: No he's just being a bastard its nothing to do with…

DANA: Stop reading in to everything

JESSICA: I'm not reading in to anything. He always has to have the upper hand on me

RUTH: It's not the upper hand he just wants to know if you're a lesbian

JESSICA: He doesn't have to ask my mates the second I go out the room

RUTH: But you haven't had sex

JESSICA: So I'm a lesbian?

RUTH: No but I mean he thinks…

JESSICA: He doesn't think anything, still like a kid thinks he is somehow better than me because he has had sex, obviously he has – he's my dad!

DANA: Jess I don't think he thinks that! Fuck's sake

JESSICA: Everyone thinks they are so much fucking better than me or grown up or something because they've had sex and I haven't

DANA: *(Soothing.)* No they don't

JESSICA: Everyone thinks the world just comes down to sex. Not even love but sex. Every soap, every book, every film, every conversation, every emotion I ever have there is always someone tracing it back to sex, the origin of everything! Even my own dad it's all come down to what I like in sex or whether he is having sex with my mum or not, or whether I've had sex

RUTH: It's not that big a deal

JESSICA: I know! I know it's not a big deal. Sex isn't a fucking big deal, I'm not embarrassed it's not like I couldn't if I wanted to, there has just been no one I've wanted to with so why would I do it? What's the point? I'm not missing out on something huge *(DANA and RUTH laughs.)* don't be like that

DANA: Look it's fine, okay okay okay you're not a lesbian we know that, you don't have to have sex to prove that you're not

JESSICA: But he fucking seems to think I do. I just, I…like I know all…It's just like just because I've never actually done it I'm an idiot or unattractive or immature or a freak or apparently a fucking lesbian! I mean the actual what ten maybe fifteen maybe even twenty minutes where you actually have sex, where you actually have a guy's dick…

DANA: Oh Jess don't

JESSICA: Why is that such a big deal? Just because I have not done one thing with one guy just once for less than a quarter of an hour everyone thinks I am somehow lacking and don't understand the absolute key to the world

DANA: To the fucking world

65

RUTH and DANA laugh again, JESSICA gives up lights another cigarette.

DANA: Relax babe just relax

JESSICA: He is staying one night, two max I'm not looking after him

JIM comes out with the food.

JIM: Interrupting? I hope so

RUTH: Oh wow look at this *(JIM puts the food down.)*

DANA: Fucking hell Jim

JIM: Well when there is no chicken one must make do

RUTH: This is amazing

JESSICA: Yeah well done dad you can use the microwave

RUTH: Jess

JIM: What have I done now?

DANA: Nothing nothing ignore her, let's all have another drink

JIM: Okay, well actually let me do this properly

JIM starts making the drinks properly.

DANA: Okay okay hands off everyone

JIM: Used to work in a bar when I was younger

RUTH: Really?

JESSICA: At a golf club

JIM: Well yes, yes but *(To RUTH and jokingly.)* it was the place to be, like the Hacienda of Chichester

RUTH: What's the Hacienda?

DANA: That Manchester club

JIM: Oh god before all your time

DANA: I watched 24 Hour Party People

JIM: What's that?

DANA: Like film about Joy Division and the Happy Mondays and Factory Records and stuff

JIM: God it's being documented you girls will find that feels very odd

RUTH: What?

JIM: I was what in my 20s, young guy just met Fiona drove up to the Hacienda just to see what all the fuss was about. God it was a nightmare. Had a knife pulled on me in the toilets, Fiona had a horrendous time, hell of a drive back but that's, that's my memories you know. That's my past. And now it's just something that's been and gone. Something recreated in an era film for kids like you to watch and say 'oh it was like that was it' and old men like me to say 'I remember that'

RUTH: You're not that old

JIM: Not that young either

JESSICA: Dad you're not that old

DANA: Don't be morbid

JIM: Sorry, I won't. All a bit pathetic. God what a loser

RUTH: You're not a loser

JIM: 'Fraid I might be

RUTH: Well if you are I am. Friday night, just been dumped at home fucking pissed

JIM: Newly single middle aged homeless man. Give me five Ruthie

They high five.

RUTH: *(Singing the Beck song.)* 'I'm a loser baby, so why don't you kill me'

JIM: You joining us Dana? Losers club?

DANA: Propositioned by a ginger ninja

JIM: Three and Jessica sweetie?

JESSICA: Yeah I'm a loser daddy happy?

JIM: – Oh Jess don't take it like that

DANA: So am I. Creepy boss in a boring job

JIM: Darling I have the edge on boring. If you haven't gone in every day for thirty-five years and seriously considered hole punching each one of my fingers just, for, something, to, do…you haven't known boredom like I have

DANA: *(Points.)* Jim you're a loser

JIM: Yes I am *(JIM goes for a high five and DANA goes for a fist bump.)* Oh what's that?

DANA: Don't worry high five

Jim and Dana high five

RUTH: Me too, me too

JIM: Done *(They all take their drinks JIM has just finished.)* Bit like magnets failures they all stick together and find each other

DANA: Yeah in some flat other side of London our counterparts

JIM: The winners

RUTH: What?

DANA: Huddled together in success

JIM: You're, what was his name, Bernie?

DANA: Ben

JIM: He's there… The winners. Your boyfriend Ruth he's there as well, Jessie everyone else is there

DANA and RUTH and JIM laugh, toasting.

JIM: To the winners of this world

DANA: Which we are not

JIM: Which we are not

DANA: To the winners

RUTH: To the winners

JESSICA: *(Grudgingly.)* to the winners

JIM: To the bloody Barrys of this world

RUTH and DANA drink not noticing JESSICA and JIM who have caught each other's eye.

SCENE THREE

Midnight. JESSICA is curled up in the cushion chair watching in slight disgust RUTH and DANA who sit either side of JIM on the sofa. Because I Got High by Afroman is playing on the ipod speakers. The girls have cigarettes and all have drinks.

DANA: 'It's like…'

DANA and RUTH: 'I don't care about nothing man'

DANA and RUTH dance with their arms up in the air either side of a bemused JIM.

JIM: Er and what's this?

RUTH: Because I Got High

JIM: My God that's the name of it?

DANA: Yeah look at it *(Gesturing to the speaker.)*

JIM: Good God

RUTH: *(Head on his shoulder.)* Aw you're so cute

JIM: Am I?

RUTH: Yup

JIM: Do you two then, so a bit of, this

RUTH: What?

JIM: Smoke cannabis

The two laugh.

DANA: She does

RUTH: So do you! Shall we Jim?

JIM: What?

RUTH: Shall we?

JIM: Sorry?

RUTH: Smoke

DANA: Ruth!

JIM: *(Nodding to JESSICA.)* I don't think so

JESSICA: *(Defiantly.)* Yeah why not?

RUTH: '*(Sings the lyric.)*'

JIM: Jessie don't be stupid

DANA: Shall we change the song?

RUTH: *(Whining.)* No

DANA turns off the music.

RUTH: Do you want some draw then?

DANA: Do you mind Jim?

JIM: No well, you, you girls do what you want

DANA laughs, RUTH gets up and goes to the bedroom.

JIM: Is that a yes then?

DANA: Yeah she's just getting some, are you gonna do some Jim?

JIM: Oh well *(Glances at JESSICA.)*

JESSICA: I am

JIM: Well I have to be honest haven't done this for years

DANA: Since the Hacienda?

JIM: *(Laughing.)* Indeed, indeed since the Hacienda

RUTH returns with her box where she keeps stuff for rolling.

RUTH: Haven't got that much probably only a couple or maybe three small

JIM: Blimey isn't that enough?

DANA: She has suffered an emotional trauma

RUTH: There are four of us smoking, *(Sits on sofa.)* you are Jess aren't you?

JESSICA: Yeah whatever

JIM: Well I don't know about this

DANA: Oh Jim it'll be so funny go on

RUTH: *(Gives him a friendly push.)* Go on, live a little. Oh my god I feel so fucking drunk

RUTH slithers off the sofa and sits on the floor, nearer the table, starts to roll.

JIM: Oh dear someone ashed in the chocolate

DANA: It's good will make us skinny

JIM: So are you a hippie now Ruth?

DANA: It's all because of Twix

RUTH: Can we not talk about him?

DANA: Thinks he is so amazing

RUTH: I don't think he is so amazing, I think he is a bastard

DANA: Like always going on about how clever he is and stuff

JESSICA: Like when she came back about the Andrex toilet
paper

DANA: Oh my god yes

RUTH: It's true! It's a valid point

DANA: Okay my God Jim listen

RUTH: Jim will agree with me

DANA: She came back like saying Twix had explained how
we can't buy Andrex because they have that like Labrador
puppy on the adverts and like, how did you explain it…

JIM: What because of animals acting in adverts?

DANA: No!

RUTH: He did say that! He did say that as well

DANA: Then what's the other reason?

RUTH: Like because like using animals in products and animal
testing and stuff

JIM: What they test Andrex on animals?

DANA: No it's like an association thing she…

RUTH: Okay basically he said and he is right that seeing an
animal associated with products means you associate
animals with a product and so if you found out that they
used animal parts or tested on animals or something then
you would find it easier to accept that it was necessary
because they are so int, intri-nic-ally linked like to human
products

DANA: See! *(DANA and JESSICA laughs, JIM hides that he is too.)*

RUTH: It's all on the internet I can show you

JESSICA: Everything is on the fucking internet

RUTH: No it had adverts for Asda on it okay! Asda wouldn't sponsor some random site

JIM: It's pretty dangerous territory the internet Ruth, all these conspiracy theories, I mean everything's a con according to them landing on the Moon, 9/11 all that

RUTH: Well I don't believe in 9/11

JESSICA: How can you not believe in it?

RUTH: No I don't like not believe in it, I know it happened. But the government you can see the building like blows up before the plane hits it

JESSICA: Oh my God

RUTH: It's not like just me Twix says it's like 20% of people believe that the government did it and there were no Jewish people died or like like only a few or something because they were all like truanting or like… like you should talk to Twix about it he can explain it all properly I'm really bad at it

JESSICA: Fucking bullshit

DANA: Bullshit

RUTH: No you don't understand. You're acting like he is some like weirdo. You like him Dana!

DANA: Yeah he's nice but he's like, you know

JESSICA: Pretentious

RUTH: He's not pretentious!

JESSICA: Come on all the protest rallies with his *(Gestures to her head, her and DANA start laughing.)*

DANA: When he dyed his hair

RUTH: That was once! He did try to dye it back you know that, that's why he cut his hair so short

DANA: Because he's got green hair now Jim

JIM: What?

DANA: He dyed it for this green party rally and he couldn't get it back to normal

RUTH: He has now, its normal now! Stop it you guys, you're making him sound so weird

JESSICA: No Ruth you know he's like fine

DANA: Yeah he is nice and everything and quite hot

JIM: Despite the green hair

RUTH: Not anymore! You just have to meet him Jim to understand they just, like I can't explain. He looks at stuff in such a different way. Like, like okay don't laugh Dana Jess don't either of you fucking dare laugh but Jim he was like 'life is like scooping water up in your hand and it trickles through leaving you only with the memory'. Like, stop laughing, you two are such bitches, like come on that is beautiful

JESSICA: Anyone can talk shit like that! Like um Dana say something, anything

DANA: What?

JESSICA: Like name something or an object like anything

RUTH: Fuck's sake

JESSICA: Like say something anything like um chopsticks or…

JIM: Life, life is like chopsticks… tricky to get right and everyone has their own way

DANA: Wow

JESSICA: Dad

RUTH: Jim how did you do that?

JIM: Jessie's right it's not that hard

RUTH: Like do another one

DANA: Jeans

JIM: Oh um, okay um jeans are like life because if you use it too much you wear them out

RUTH: What the fuck! Wow! You would love Twix

DANA: Oh yeah *(She lies on the sofa, puts her feet on JIM.)* fucking love him. He hates everything

RUTH: No he doesn't

JIM: Sounds much more like you Jessie

DANA and RUTH laugh, JESSICA tightens up again.

DANA: He's anti-meat, anti-fur, anti-animal testing…

RUTH: Oh sorry he doesn't like animals being murdered how fucking controversial

DANA: Anti-conservative, anti-labour, anti-capitalism, anti-socialism, anti-democracy

RUTH: They are all fucking liars okay? This is a bit of a fucked up zoot

DANA: Oh Jesus Ruth that's like a fucking child's done it

RUTH: Well don't shout at me when I'm doing it, shall I spark it?

DANA: If you can

RUTH: *(Lights it.)* It's fine you just have to be careful with it, there it's fine, Jess take it while I do another

JESSICA takes it and smokes, JIM glares.

JESSICA: Stop playing the victim and grow some balls, go on stop me I dare you

RUTH looks shocked, DANA laughs.

JIM: Don't you speak to me like that

JESSICA: You don't want to be spoken to like that, get out of my flat

JIM: Rented with my money

JESSICA: No with my money

JIM: Going to pay me back then?

JESSICA: Oh sorry I forgot I'm permanently in debt to mum and you for even having me?

JIM: Bit of gratitude wouldn't go amiss

JESSICA: Or maybe it's mum and Barry I'm in debt to

JIM: You watch it now Jessica

RUTH: Who's Barry?

JESSICA: Is that what the fucking problem is?

DANA: Oh my God shut up Jess, give me that *(Taking the joint.)*

RUTH: *(To JIM.)* Ignore her, she's drunk. We're all a bit drunk

JIM: True, true

DANA: *(Passing him his drink.)* Drink up

JIM: *(Smiles at DANA.)* Very bad advice

DANA: I specialise in that

RUTH: Who's Barry?

JESSICA: Doesn't matter

RUTH: Oh sorry is it like…

JIM: No no it's fine go on then Jessie why don't you enjoy yourself

JESSICA: It doesn't matter

RUTH: I didn't mean to…

JIM: No sorry I'm not having a go at you Ruthie dear, it's just um well Fiona didn't just throw me out I've um, well been replaced

RUTH: Oh shit

JIM: Yes um so well Barry is her new, well…

DANA: You don't have to tell us

RUTH: What a bitch

DANA: Yeah that's really fucking low

RUTH: Such a bitch

JIM: Yes well he's a bit younger than her too not by all that much to be quite fair I suppose

RUTH gets up and sits on the sofa as DANA slides off onto the floor to check the box for more weed, she then turns on the floor and faces him on the sofa, legs crossed looking up at him. RUTH smoking the joint, puts her hand on his knee. JESSICA sulks.

DANA: That's horrible

RUTH: Such a bitch

JIM: Was the um, the roofer actually as a bit um of a cliché, sounds all a bit Adrian Mole really

RUTH: Fiona's such a bitch

JIM: Got him in to sort out some cracked tiles and well he did a bit more than that

DANA: The cunt

JIM: Told me today. I don't know why Jessie you have to say those things because he hasn't exactly been around for twenty years

JESSICA: Twenty one

JIM: What?

JESSICA: I'm twenty one daddy

DANA: Can you leave him alone, he's upset

JIM: No it's okay girls. All a bit of a shock but yes came home, Fiona was there waiting for me, which I thought was a bit odd. Then said it wasn't working and I asked why and she said because I no longer 'was the man she used to know' I mean really how typical can you get. But I suppose you always expect things to be different but they actually are always like a bloody Eastenders episode

RUTH: Yeah me and Twix before was just like that I mean he said 'I don't think we can go on like this for that much longer' and I was like you are so fucking clichéd but its...

DANA: Go on Jim

JIM: Yes well total cliché and I start to get a bit het up, I mean we both did and Barry comes out of the kitchen and says I better leave and it all rather kicked off and then Jessie came home to a bit of a scrum

JESSICA: You crying on the stairs

JIM: Well...

RUTH: *(Mouthing.)* Shut up

DANA: I'm so sorry Jim *(Patting his legs.)*

RUTH: And she just threw you out!?

JIM: Well um I suppose so

RUTH: I never liked Fiona

DANA: Any woman that does that is a total...I mean for fuck's sake, how long have you been married?

JIM: Twenty six years

RUTH: What a bitch

DANA: She's a fucking cunt not worth a second of your time, you stay here

RUTH: She's a bitch

JIM: I suppose

RUTH: Do you want the end? *(Offers the joint.)*

JIM: Oh well I dunno

RUTH: We're gonna have another

DANA: Yeah go on

JIM: *(Nervously takes the joint.)* I suppose *(He is upset but also rather enjoying the attention.)*

RUTH: Don't think anything more of her. She is a bitch

DANA: You could do way better

RUTH: She's a nasty cunt no one should ever cheat

JESSICA: Okay for fuck's sake can you guys shut up

DANA: Okay sorry but come on

RUTH: Yeah Jess come on she's been such a bitch

JESSICA: I haven't said she was right but can you stop it, that's my mum

RUTH: Jess you don't understand you can't cheat on people in relationships it's the worst thing you could do

JESSICA: Can you go and fuck yourself, seriously?

RUTH: Oh my God can you stop getting so pissy with me

JIM: Hey girls girls stop I don't want a fight on my account. Be a good girl Ruth and pass me a drink

DANA: We're just really sorry Jim

JIM: That's very sweet of you both

RUTH: Shall we put some music on?

JIM: Yeah go on

RUTH leans over to the ipod and starts looking.

DANA: I really am so sorry Jim, shall we spark the other one?

JIM: Might as well go the whole hog

JESSICA: I can't stand the smell

DANA: *(Gets the other joint, shares it with JIM.)* Go on

JESSICA opens the window.

RUTH: Some dubstep

DANA: Ruth that's all so over

RUTH: Me and Twix like it

DANA: There is no you and Twix

RUTH: Shut up!

DANA: Sorry was less harsh in my head

JIM: Girls deep breathe, claws in, big smiles okay? So what's this Twix look like?

RUTH: Shall I show him to you?

JIM: And how are you going to do that?

RUTH gets up and walks off to her room, hands JESSICA the joint.

DANA: Oh she's gone

JIM starts laughing and then so does DANA, the two get a bit hysterical, JESSICA watches, she walks over to the window and throws the rest of the joint out, she closes it, she stands there and watches the pair laugh

JIM: Just get… *(Can't say it laughs.)*

DANA: It's like…bye

They laugh more, they clutch each other.

DANA: I want to ask you something, both of you

JIM: Go for it sweetheart

DANA: Is it bad that I get bored kissing people?

JIM: Sorry what?

DANA: I mean like I can be kissing, like…

RUTH returns zig zagging with her laptop.

DANA: Oh, oh she's back

They laugh more, RUTH shoves herself in between them.

DANA: No like I can be mid-kissing someone then my mind like wanders off and I get really bored and I just think oh Jesus how long am I going to have to do this for

JIM: What?

DANA: I know that's bad isn't it

JIM: You need to have better kissers

RUTH: Jim? Jim? *(He gives her mock full attention, DANA starts off laughing again, so does JIM, RUTH's out of it barely notices.)* This is his Facebook

JIM: Like the, the film

RUTH: What?

JIM: The Facebook film

RUTH: What?

JIM: *(Turns to DANA.)* The, the Facebook film

DANA: The Facebook film?

JIM: Yes that that

RUTH: What?

DANA: *(Explaining to RUTH.)* Facebook like in the Facebook film

RUTH: The Facebook film?

DANA: Yeah the Facebook film

JESSICA: The Social Network

DANA and JIM: Yes!

RUTH: Oh yeah, like…yeah

JIM: Sorry go on

RUTH: Hang on music *(She puts on* Please Mr Postman *by The Marvelettes but the Cragga dubstep version.)*

JIM: Oh God you listen to this kind of music, I thought this would be terribly out of date or are you being ironic?

RUTH: Oh no it's not like you think

JIM: No?

DANA: No wait Jim wait, hang on

JIM: For what?

DANA: *(Holding on to him, the two cling to each other waiting.)* You'll love it, turn it up Ruth up turn it up… *(The dubstep starts.)* see? *(They start laughing, kind of manically.)*

RUTH: Hang on let me find a good photo

JIM: Oh god, oh god I feel really sick

DANA laughs more, so does JIM.

DANA: Laughing makes you higher

JIM: Fuck

RUTH: Can you pay attention?

JIM: Sorry, sorry

DANA: Bad boy

RUTH: There *(Shows them a photo, they stare for a bit in silence.)*

JIM: He looks a bit like a, like a, like a really, really pale horse

They look a bit closer, DANA starts laughing so does JIM, RUTH stares closer. JIM and DANA come off the sofa and closer together laughing very hard. JESSICA watches. DANA comes closer, she puts her fingers on his lips trying to shush him even though she is laughing too.

RUTH: *(Upset.)* No he doesn't

This just sets them off harder.

DANA: You're such a bad boy

JIM: *(Drawing himself up.)* I'm old enough to be your father

DANA: Oh my God I just thought of something

JIM: What?

She can't say it for laughing, he can't ask.

JIM: What?

DANA: I just thought…

JIM: What?

DANA: You *are* her father

DANA points over to JESSICA, they all look over at her fuming by the window, RUTH on her laptop, JIM and DANA on the floor, RUTH, DANA and JIM all start laughing hysterically.

SCENE FOUR

1am. DANA and JIM sit facing each other on the sofa.

DANA: It's just like, he is kind of good-looking

JIM: Mm

DANA: I mean you know who cares, everyone does stupid things to…

JIM: To get to the top

DANA: To get to the top, yeah exactly

JIM: Of course

DANA: I mean I swear it happens like all the time

JIM: Yup

DANA: I mean like loads of people sleep with someone for a job or whatever and it doesn't make them...

JIM: No no of course not

DANA: I mean it's not like he is some old fat like whatever. I mean I know he is ginger but I do kind of fancy him

JIM: Mm

DANA: But I like might have anyway

JIM: Yeah

DANA: Not that I'm a slut or anything but you know

JIM: No, no

DANA: Like Jim you are so amazing, like talking to me like this, thank you. I don't know why Jess is so mean to you, you are amazing.

JIM: Oh sweetheart

DANA: No seriously, it's so good to have like an adult's opinion

JIM: Christ am I the adult?

DANA: Yeah well you know what I mean, I know I am and everything but still

JIM: No well what's it they say? Um, growing old, growing old is mandatory growing up is optional

DANA: *(Laughs.)* Do they?

JIM: It's true

DANA: Do you think I'm being really childish?

JIM: No no sweetheart I just mean, oh I don't really know what I mean

DANA: I don't know if I think it's just a good idea because I'm drunk

JIM: Well it's not a 'good' idea

DANA: No well no… *(Laughs embarrassed.)* no

JIM: But you know you are a grown up you can make your own decisions

DANA: Yeah…yeah I suppose

DANA pauses thinking, bites her lip. JIM watches.

JIM: You know you think you are going to have that magic moment, when you just are a responsible adult. That click moment and you always think it's just round the corner but well…mine's still coming

DANA: Yeah, I dunno I just thought like 18, well like 18 and have left school, or like left uni

JIM: Or when you got your first job? Or moved out? Or lived alone? Or got married and had kids?

DANA: *(Laughing.)* I suppose

JIM: Never comes darling, all you have to do is make the decision in front of you

DANA: Yeah?

JIM: Yes. Look Dana you are young, free, beautiful…

DANA: Oh Jim shut up

JIM: And you aren't tied down to some boy or place or house or anything, do what you want to do

DANA: I wish you were my dad

They laugh.

DANA: Thank you, thanks Jim

DANA gives JIM a kiss on the cheek, RUTH comes out of the kitchen eating Percy Pig sweets.

DANA: *(Gets up.)* I'm going to go check on Jess

JIM: Okay sweetheart but I'd leave her to it

DANA: No I'll check

DANA stumbles out and RUTH comes over.

JIM: Hello darling come for your open heart session?

RUTH: Huh?

JIM: Seem to have been mistaken for an agony aunt tonight

RUTH: Oh I'm sorry about her

JIM: No don't you worry yourself, only wish Jessie would buck up

RUTH: You know what she's like she doesn't mean it

JIM: Fear she does

RUTH: No she's just in a mood

JIM: Perhaps

RUTH: She should be nice to you especially after everything

JIM: After what?

RUTH: ...Fiona

JIM: Oh that's alright, it's you know, nothing

RUTH: Maybe it's for the best

JIM: I suspect

RUTH: My mum always said you two didn't get on

JIM: Hm?

RUTH: My mum. She always said you know Mr and Mrs Bank fight tooth and nail, or claw. Whatever that expression is

JIM: Oh well. No we didn't. Probably seemed like that, to her, to Jessie even but well…I suppose we did have our moments but, but, but…c'est la vie

RUTH: Yeah

JIM: C'est la vie… ma petit souris

RUTH: Little mouse?

JIM: Oui, oui. Ma petit souris tu *(Gestures trying to find the word for will.)* dans la future connais c'est la vie, c'est la vie

RUTH: *(Reaches for their drinks and passes one to JIM, clinking glasses with him.)* C'est la vie

JIM: Et avec votre petit homme, Monsieur Twix, il est rien

RUTH: Rien?

JIM: Nothing

RUTH: Nothing

JIM: Rien. Il est rien et stupide et doit avoir une petit *(Doesn't know the word but demonstrates.)* une très très petit là *(Points to his trousers, RUTH laughs.)* en bas, en bas

DANA comes out the bedroom she has a coat on.

RUTH: Where's Jess?

DANA: I dunno

JIM: I thought you were checking on her

DANA: No no fuck that, fuck it. I'm going to see Ben

RUTH: What? Dana no what?

JIM: Ben?

DANA: Is it still raining?

RUTH: No you really shouldn't go

DANA: I am

RUTH: This is a bad idea

DANA: Why?

RUTH: You're like, like fucked, wait

DANA: No I won't want to in the morning

JIM: Oh the, the…

RUTH: Boss

DANA: Yeah, *(Brushing her hair.)* shall I go Jim?

JIM: Your decision darling

RUTH: No don't

DANA: No fuck it, where's my, my *(Looking around.)* …feet

JIM: Your feet?

DANA: You know what I mean

JIM: They're there *(Laughs at his own joke.)*

DANA: I mean, my, my…you know

RUTH: Dana

DANA: No fuck it, ah here they are *(Finds her shoes and puts them on.)*

RUTH: Dana

DANA: No stop trying to put me off. I am like happy to do it now, I like him I feel like it and if I wait for later or the morning or you keep talking I won't want to so I'm just going okay so stop. Just going to get a cab there and like yeah

JIM: God you lot are so, exciting

DANA: I need some cash

RUTH: You're being a prostitute

DANA: Oh fuck off where's some cash?

RUTH: *(Getting up.)* Look I'm going to get Jess

JIM: Oh that's right get the law involved

RUTH: No because I'm like fucked and this is a, this isn't a good idea

DANA: No look like seriously Ruth I don't care about these kind of things you know, you know what I mean. You like care about things. You really care about shit like anti-fur and anti-meat and stuff

RUTH: That's not really…

DANA: But I just don't really care about stuff

RUTH: You do

DANA: No I don't I'm, I'm kind of shallow, like I like love Simon Cowell and Eastenders and I don't like reading and I don't think about death and God and stuff I just you know, I don't care about stuff and sex might be this big like thing to you but it's just you know, whatever

RUTH: What because you watch X Factor you are going to sleep with someone for a job

DANA: No look I'm going *(She is ready and leaving.)* And I'm borrowing your umbrella

RUTH: That's not mine

DANA: Then I'm borrowing whoever's umbrella that is

RUTH: No Dana

DANA: You weren't listening to what I said, you don't understand

RUTH: No look…

DANA: Look just trust me. It's okay isn't it Jim?

JIM: It's your life

DANA: Yeah. I'm going

RUTH: No where did Jess go? Don't Dana

DANA: No I'm gone

RUTH: No but Dana

DANA: Gone

RUTH: This isn't…

DANA: Bye

DANA shuts the door and is gone.

JIM: Never mind darling

RUTH: It's not a good idea

JIM: You did your best

RUTH: Yeah

JIM: She's a grown girl can make her own decisions

RUTH: Yeah but she, I'm trying to…Jess won't be happy

JIM: God how did I have such a killjoy for a daughter *(JESSICA comes out.)* Are your ears burning?

JESSICA: I'm going to go to the bathroom

JIM: Yes I'm sure how many times have you been?

JESSICA: We've been drinking since like nine thirty. Where's Dana?

RUTH: Um *(JIM makes a face about JESSICA, she starts to giggle.)* never you mind

JESSICA: What?

JIM: Shall we put the music back on?

JESSICA: Where's…

RUTH: Yeah that's a good idea

JIM: Music! Music!

JESSICA: Alright fine whatever, I don't care

JIM jumps up and looks through the music, JESSICA slams the door into the bathroom, JIM and RUTH laugh at her temper.

JIM: *(About the music.)* Christ you have this?

RUTH: What? *(RUTH's phone goes.)* Shit he's texted me!

JIM: Haven't heard this for years!

JIM plays Let's Get It On *by Marvin Gaye*

JIM: *(In exaggerated mime behind the sofa.)* 'I've been really trying baby'

RUTH reading the text, noticing he isn't being watched JIM moves back to the sofa, as he sits on the sofa next to her he tries the mime again.

JIM: *(Mime again.)* 'Come on, oh come on'

RUTH looks to him tries to laugh but starts crying.

JIM: Hey love sorry oh sorry…was it from the eh, the um boyfriend *(RUTH nods.)* ah well come on…not too bad… only boys you know, only boys…Sweetheart, he doesn't deserve you, anyone that makes you feel like this…same boat here darling same boat…I'm sorry, don't worry… don't cry

JESSICA comes out of the bathroom, sees RUTH crying she goes forward to comfort but JIM puts his hand up stopping her.

JESSICA: *(Mouthing to JIM.)* My friend

JIM: *(Mouthing back.)* Leave it

JESSICA makes another little move towards RUTH but JIM repeats shooing her away.

JESSICA: *(About the music, mouthing.)* What the fuck is this?

JIM shrugs it off, RUTH hasn't seen any of this. JESSICA exits.

JIM: What did he say?

RUTH: Just saying how miserable I've made him

JIM: Oh how horrible

RUTH: I don't want him to do anything bad

JIM: Oh he won't he won't, just you know everyone's overdramatic when they're upset

RUTH: Yeah

JIM: Jessie went through a phase when she was 15 whenever we fought where she would write on her bedroom door, we had that little white board remember? It would either say she was going to kill herself or she was going to kill me, it alternated by week, either way it was apparently going to be my fault

RUTH laughs a little.

JIM: Come on love… *(He rocks her a bit to the music.)* good song isn't it? *(RUTH half-laughs.)* Oh yes that's right laugh at my musical ineptitude

RUTH: *(Sitting up.)* Sorry

JIM: It's alright

As RUTH wipes her face JIM bobs his head to the rhythm of the song.

RUTH: Is that your dad dancing?

JIM: An aprox, approximation of it, Jesus I can't speak

RUTH: God can't believe you smoked

JIM: I know

RUTH gets up reaching for tissues.

RUTH: It's just mad

JIM: *(Also standing.)* Yes well

RUTH sniffs.

JIM: Oh come here love

JIM hugs her.

RUTH: Sorry

JIM: It's fine

RUTH: I'm ruining your night

JIM: Well it was never going to be a good night was it, for either of us

RUTH: You're an agony aunt again

JIM: No sweetheart no, not with you. You're little Ruthie from number 5

RUTH: Little Ruthie?

JIM: Indeed

RUTH: No, stop rocking

JIM: Dad dancing

RUTH laughs again, they are still hugging.

JIM: There we go, nice smile on your face

RUTH: God you're fucked

JIM: So are you

RUTH: That's true

JIM: *(Sings a lyric of the song.)*

RUTH smiles and JIM playing the fool takes her hand and spins her round, they dance and RUTH cheers up, it's a bit drunken and pathetic but there is something sweet about it, JESSICA comes out of her bedroom at the sound of laughter and watches.

SCENE FIVE

3am. JIM sits watching the TV, it's a children's channel. He finds the remote and tries to change it, the TV fuzzes and starts making an odd noise. He looks around, fiddles with the remote to no avail. He gets up and goes to the TV, he can't sort it out, he presses something it blasts loud David Attenborough. He panics and pulls the plug out of the wall and sits as JESSICA comes in.

JESSICA: What are you doing?

JIM: Nothing

JESSICA: Thought I heard the TV

JIM: Imagining things love

JESSICA: Ruth gone to bed now?

JIM: Well she's gone to her room I don't know if she's gone to sleep

JESSICA: I can't sleep

JIM: Neither can I, must be all that stuff from earlier

JESSICA: You feel okay?

JIM: Yeah, yeah, just a bit, fuzzed, no well I'm drunk

JESSICA: Same

JIM: Past that tired barrier thing

JESSICA: Same

JESSICA sits.

JESSICA: Feel a bit sick

JIM: Toilet's right there

JESSICA: I'm not going to be sick, I just feel sick

JIM: Oh okay

JESSICA: Don't you?

JIM: What?

JESSICA: Feel…oh never mind

They sit in silence.

JESSICA: You not going to say anything?

JIM: What do you want me to say?

JESSICA: I don't want you to say anything

JIM: Then why do you say 'are you not going to speak to me then'

JESSICA: I didn't say that I said 'are you not going to say anything'

JIM: Same difference

JESSICA: No it's not because if I said 'are you not going to talk to me' that's being really aggressive I just said 'are you not going to say anything' because we were sitting in silence

JIM: It's not up to me to start a conversation

JESSICA: And it's not up to me

JIM: But you are the one that starts criticising it

JESSICA: Well I'm sorry you find it hard to 'make' fucking conversation with me

JIM: You do swear a hell of a lot Jessie

JESSICA: *(Giving up.)* Oh for God's sake

Pause again.

JIM: How's the job hunting going?

JESSICA sighs and looks away from him.

JIM: What? *(No response.)* Fine don't talk to me then

JESSICA: I'm not not talking to you

JIM: You going to answer my question?

JESSICA: You asked me it like ten times on the way down here you know the answer

JIM: I am trying to make conversation like you wanted

JESSICA: What do you mean like I wanted?

JIM: Because you were complaining about sitting in silence

JESSICA: I didn't know it was such an effort why are you treating me like a fucking stranger

JIM: I wouldn't put up with this from a fucking stranger

JESSICA: You don't just have to sit down and ask a string of questions to keep me happy

JIM: If I didn't you would say I don't know anything about you

JESSICA: Dad if you just looked on my Facebook you would know more than you ever have

JIM: And that's why I ask about job hunting but apparently that isn't right

JESSICA: Because you've already fucking asked me that! And I told you that I am still looking! Leave. It.

JIM: Then we can just sit in silence again

JESSICA: *(After a slight pause.)* Why can't we talk about something important?

JIM: Your job hunting is pretty important money doesn't just magically appear you know

JESSICA: Talk about mum or something

JIM: Look Jess I'm not a modern man off the tele who's going to sit down and cry and then discuss my wardrobe you know, it's fine, I'm fine, leave it

JESSICA: Fine fine I'll leave it because why should I care? Why should we talk?

JIM: Do you know how fucking tiring it is to have you constantly trying to change me?

JESSICA pauses, slightly struck by the thought, JIM is amazed by his success.

JIM: *(Trying to push his advantage.)* You can always give it out but never take it Jess

JESSICA: Well I find it pretty fucking tiring that you always just go 'I'm not perfect, hands up admit it' and then do fuck all to change

JIM: All this pathetic swearing is pretty childish didn't you get a good enough education to be able to string a sentence together without swearing

JESSICA: You swear

JIM: Not constantly like you, you'd put a sailor to shame

JESSICA: I think it's pretty childish for you to grab on to some tiny fucking aspect *(JIM reacts to the swearing.)* tiny aspect then tiny aspect; it's a habit okay? But you just did it again you won't listen to what I'm saying because you are too busy trying to win the upper hand

JIM: Okay go on then what is your point

JESSICA: That you are a fucking bastard and we hate each other and we should just leave it there you cunt

JIM: Fine, fine

Pause, they both drink.

JIM: I don't actually hate you, I may not like you very much a lot of the time but I do love you

JESSICA: I hate you

JIM: Oh Jess don't start again

JESSICA looks like she might cry.

JIM: Oh don't be upset love *(Puts his arm around her, laughing.)* I think you may love me really

JESSICA: *(Pushing him off.)* Well I'm glad that you are really listening to what I'm saying, really taking in how I feel

JIM: You are saying that you hate me Jess and now telling me off for not being nice about it. You are relentless

JESSICA: I'm so sorry! I'm so relentless in trying to fix our fucking relationship there must be something so inherently wrong with me

JIM: Yes you are an unsatisfiable sadist

Long pause, JESSICA lights a cigarette and puts down the packet, JIM reaches towards it.

JIM: Do you mind?

JESSICA shakes her head, he gets a cigarette but has difficulty lighting it, JESSICA reaches over and does it for him.

JIM: Thank you love

JESSICA: *(Reciting.)* Over the hills,
    Over the sky,
    Over the moon and sun,
    She flies,
    Her lean legs outstretched.
    Nobody to help her,
    No one to care for her,
    Nobody to tame her,
    No one to ride her.
    To put a bit in her mouth,
    Bruise her back with a saddle,
    Nobody to care for
    The wild, wild horse

JIM: Who wrote that?

JESSICA: *(Disappointed.)* Me

JIM: Really?

JESSICA: Yeah

JIM: Not bad. When did you write it?

JESSICA: When I was 10

JIM: Not bad. *(Slight pause.)* You don't like horses

JESSICA: That's not the point

JIM: Then what is the point?

JESSICA: Doesn't matter

JIM: Sorry didn't understand your bloody horse poem was there some deep down inner meaning that I missed? Jessica? Go on then what's the matter now?

JESSICA: The point is that you didn't even realise I wrote it

JIM: Was a good ten years ago you wrote that!

JESSICA: And it's still pinned up in the fucking kitchen

JIM: What?

JESSICA: It's on the notice board in your kitchen

JIM: No it's not

JESSICA: It's in the middle

JIM: Never seen it in my life

JESSICA: You laminated it

JIM: I don't know what the hell you are on about

JESSICA: You check and you'll see

JIM: How! How will I check Jess I can't go back to that kitchen, into that kitchen or near that notice board or that house ever again, remember?

JESSICA: And whose fault is that?

JIM: Barry's

JESSICA: No dad it's yours for being such a pathetic coward all the time

JIM: Jessie I know, by now, that you think I'm a loser

JESSICA: Because you are and you don't even fight that you just revel in it

JIM: What? What's this now?

JESSICA: Can't you just be a fucking man! A grown-up actual man not this stupid act, pretending you're some cute, bumbling, pathetic wash out. Just be a fucking real man, take the risk.

JIM: Well I'm sorry I'm such an enormous disappointment but you know what Jessica you settled long enough ago to be unhappy with everything I did

JESSICA: And you settled with us never getting on

JIM: Okay guilty guilty I raise my hands

JESSICA: Well don't raise your hands, fucking fight. Fight for something in your fucking life don't just raise your hands and sit and cry on stairs and get drunk with fucking twenty-year-olds. You won't fight for me you wouldn't fight for mum

JIM: Jessica I know your mother very well and it would do no good having some blazing row with her would not change her mind

JESSICA: You didn't even try

JIM: There is no point

JESSICA: You just gave up. You just left, you just left the house

JIM: What you wanted me to stay? Have some bloody ménage a trois living arrangement with them no thank you Jessica no thank you

JESSICA: You just sat there, you just fucking sat there

JIM: I am allowed to handle this exactly how I want to I'm
sorry I don't meet your requirements Jessie. This is exactly
the problem with all this feminist shit there is a whole
generation of women like you that have got more balls
than men and then beat a perfectly normal man like me up
because I don't meet your criteria

JESSICA: Yeah that's right let's wander away from reality the
more cerebral and general we can get the better this it's
about you fucking growing up

JIM: You talk to me about growing up! You are twenty years
old…

JESSICA: Twenty-one

JIM: Twenty-one-years-old without a job living off savings
thinking…

JESSICA: That's my fucking business

JIM: No it's not Jess no it's not! You know when I left
university that was it I had my own life I was an adult
but you haven't. You won't, you won't grow up and face
reality! Me and Fiona…

JESSICA: Oh you and mum what?

JIM: Oh you are a nasty piece of work my girl

JESSICA: I am fucking happy for mum, she found someone
that cares more about her than reading the Sunday papers.
I only let you come back here because mum begged me,
begged me

JIM: Jesus you really are a fucking little selfish girl. So I'm
only here because Fiona begged you, good to know. Not
because I'm your dad? Does that mean nothing to you?

JESSICA: Me being your daughter means nothing to you

JIM: Ah because you know everything, you can read my mind? That's a very special skill you have there Jessie you need to let MI5 know about that

JESSICA: You deserve nothing more than being kicked out by her and Barry, live on the street you bastard for all I care

JIM: I'm ashamed of you, you are exactly like Fiona you know that, exactly. You look like her, speak like her and you are a selfish, self-righteous, nasty bitch just like her and think you are so much better than everyone else

JESSICA: Oh I am so sorry I am like the woman you have been married to for twenty-five years!

JIM: Twenty-six years

JESSICA: Oh my God you don't win the point because I got a number wrong

JIM: Win the point? You think this is a game? You're more caught up in your own feelings than anything else! You public school self-righteous…

RUTH comes out from the corridor, heading for the bathroom trying to be quiet, but seeing them move she freezes.

JESSICA: Oh I'm public schooled is that the problem?

JIM: Sitting here in your London flat with your troubled cool friends drinking too much, smoking 'zoots'…

JESSICA: 'Smoking zoots!'

JIM: Marijuana whatever you want to bloody well call it

JESSICA: Oh daddy you're going to fit right into the new bachelor world

JIM: Oh because you have all the answers so easy for you, aren't you absolutely wonderful Jessie? Wouldn't any man be proud to be your father, wouldn't any guy be lucky to be your husband, oh that's right no one will even sleep with you

RUTH decides it's best to sneak back to her room.

JESSICA: *(Absolutely losing it.)* Shut up. Shut up. I hate you, I hate you, I just hate you so fucking much

JIM spots RUTH, he looks shocked, JESSICA turns and sees her.

RUTH: I'm just going to the bathroom, sorry was going to piss myself

JIM: *(Sweet and lovely.)* Oh no don't worry sweetheart go on

JESSICA seeing him be nice, dissolves into tears and sits and curls up on the sofa, bawling.

JIM: *(To RUTH.)* Don't worry, she's just a little bit drunk

RUTH: I know fuck, we all are

JIM: Don't worry, I'll sort it

RUTH goes into the bathroom, JIM waits till she has shut the door, sits next to JESSICA and pulls her over so she sits kneeling facing him, all the fight's gone out of her.

JIM: I'm sorry, I'm sorry I didn't want to embarrass you anymore

JESSICA: *(Crying and pathetic.)* See you always care about embarrassment

JIM: No I didn't want to make it worse for you, I'm sorry, I'm sorry sweetheart

JIM pulls her over in what is meant to be a hug, it should have been a hug, but they miss slightly and he kisses her on the forehead. She hugs him and goes face to face to speak

JESSICA: I don't want…

JIM: Oh it's alright love, it's alright

He puts his hands on her face and kisses her forehead again then on the lips. They stop. That didn't feel right. They aren't looking at each other. JESSICA leans forward so JIM can put his arms around her

again as she rests on his chest but she isn't crying, JESSICA looking at the floor and JIM at the ceiling. After a moment JESSICA gets up and half goes towards the bathroom

JESSICA: I'm just… *(Door locked, remembering RUTH is in there.)* Oh fuck

JIM: Fiona…

JESSICA: Jessica

JIM: Jessica…

JESSICA: *(Pause, lost for words.)* Fuck you

JESSICA goes off down the corridor.

JIM: *(Calling after her.)* I was only trying to be nice. *(More to himself.)* Hysterical fucking…

Key in the door, JIM turns. DANA enters the front door, soaked.

DANA: Oh hi Jim

JIM: Christ look at the state of you, what's got into you all tonight? There something in the water?

DANA: Are Jess or Ruth around?

JIM: Um Ruth's in the bathroom and um…no Jess gone to uh…

DANA: Fuck *(She goes to the sofa and sits.)*

JIM: Need to get a vicar round do an exorcism or something. Didn't you have an umbrella? You are soaking

DANA: I forgot it on the way back

JIM: Oh okay should have got a taxi then

DANA: I did

JIM: How come you're so wet?

DANA: Had to wait for ages to get one

JIM: Everything alright love?

DANA: Yeah course *(Tries to smile.)* Might put on a bit of *(TV.)*…you know

DANA tries the remote it doesn't work, she goes up to it she can't work out what's wrong.

Oh for fuck's sake, fuck, what's wrong with the fucking… *(Almost starts to cry, stops battling the TV, JIM doesn't know what to do.)*

JIM: Shall I leave you?

DANA: No it's fine, I just can't, it doesn't…

JIM: I think I might um might head to bed though

DANA: Oh okay night night, sorry night Jim

JIM leaves and goes into the corridors, DANA sees the TV's not plugged in.

DANA: Oh for fuck's sake

DANA gives up, goes back to the sofa, not sure whether to cry or not, JIM cautiously returns he goes to speak but is too awkward, he pushes something over on the desk to make a noise but DANA doesn't react, he steps forward.

JIM: Um I'm meant to be sleeping on that sofa darling just remembered

DANA: What?

JIM: I um…can't really leave you alone I um…

DANA: Oh shit sorry

RUTH's phone on the table starts ringing, JIM looks at it.

DANA: That's Ruth's

JIM: *(Reading off the phone.)* Twix

DANA: Oh

JIM: Who?

DANA: Her boyfriend

JIM: Oh yes

DANA: Shit, she in her room?

JIM: Oh yes think so, no wait bathroom

JIM knocks on the bathroom door.

JIM: Ruthie?

RUTH: What?

JIM: That Twix is calling you

RUTH: Fuck okay

JIM: *(JIM sits.)* Damn it *(He pours himself another drink.)*

RUTH appears half in tracksuits now, pulling on a top.

RUTH: Sorry Jim wanted to get out of my jeans and stuff was really… *(The phone stops ringing.)* fuck

DANA: You missed it

RUTH: Yeah

DANA: Call him

RUTH picks up the phone, DANA sits in the cushions.

RUTH: No fuck him. I mean if he wants me he can call back again, yeah? Right?

DANA: Yeah okay whatever

RUTH: That's right isn't it Jim?

JIM: Sorry?

RUTH: He wants me he can call back

JIM: Yeah

RUTH: *(Putting her phone down, looks at DANA.)* Shit you're back

DANA: What?

RUTH: You're back, that was quick!

DANA: Yeah

RUTH: So what happened? *(DANA shrugs.)* That's not an answer. Was he really shit?

DANA: No he was fine

RUTH: I told you it wasn't a good idea. Does Jess know you're back?

DANA: Haven't seen her

RUTH: Oh shit I don't think she even knows where you went. You going to tell her?

DANA: I don't care

RUTH: What's the matter with you?

DANA: Nothing

JESSICA emerges.

JESSICA: Look…shit hey I thought you'd gone to bed, why are you all wet?

RUTH: Twix just called me again but he can call me again right? I mean if he wants to speak to me he can call back yeah?

JESSICA: Yeah I suppose. Why are you wet? Have you been out?

RUTH: Dana just saw Ben

JESSICA: What?

RUTH: Have you got buyer's remorse?

JESSICA: What do you mean you went to go and see him?

RUTH: She fucked him? Didn't you Dana?

JESSICA: Yeah?

RUTH: Yeah

DANA: Yeah

JESSICA: Fucking hell

RUTH: You little slut

DANA: Thanks

JESSICA: Do you wish you hadn't?

DANA: He sacked me too

RUTH: What?

DANA: I don't want to talk about it

JIM: He slept with you then sacked you, that's illegal isn't it?

DANA: Well I'm sure it's not legal for me to sleep with him for a job in the first place…he gave me some money at the end and I took it

JESSICA: What? Why?

DANA: Because he sacked me I need money don't I?

JESSICA: Are you fucking crazy?

DANA: Well what else am I meant to do?

RUTH: *(Laughing.)* You're such a little whore

JESSICA: Ignore her she's drunk

RUTH: You are a little slut it's disgusting

JIM: Christ cat fight

DANA: Can you just leave me alone?

RUTH: You need some self-respect, to love yourself

DANA: That's my fucking problem, you think you know everything. That's my fucking problem.

RUTH: What?

DANA: That is my problem. I love myself, I love myself way too fucking much

JESSICA: Fucks sake Dan'

DANA: I'm trying to be truthful! I can't help it, I love how sexy I am and how guys look at me

RUTH: You are such an arrogant…

DANA: Yeah I know that's what I'm saying okay? It's not self-respect problems. I don't need to learn 'to love myself' I need to fucking hate myself I need to fucking divorce myself!

RUTH: You're talking shit, if you let people use you…

DANA: No that's it they aren't using me I'm using them. I look at a guy in a club and think I'll have that one or someone's looking at me on the tube and I think I'll fuck you around and like smile at them and send them crazy and stuff it's not self respect. I just want, like I need people to confirm that its true like what I know is true what fucking has to be true. I'm not being a slut I'm not doing it because I enjoy it it's like, like validating my parking you know *(JIM and JESSICA start laughing.)* is that really fucked up?

JESSICA: Yeah that's so fucked up *(DANA smiles.)*

RUTH: That's just weird

DANA: Because you are the fucking expert because you and Twix the twat love each other

RUTH: Yeah actually

DANA: Yeah 'kay until you have someone else or someone after that. And even now you won't pick up his calls, everyone fucking thinks it's special for them. I've just got the clear sight to say fuck all that, sex is just sex it doesn't matter and it doesn't matter if it's a stranger or your precious pretentious little boyfriend

RUTH: Oh wait sorry because you're not just a whore you're doing it because of deep-rooted insecurity, I see

RUTH's phone rings again.

DANA: Oh is that Twix? Better get it. Second time and everything *(Ruth rolls her eyes and reaches for it.)* Hurry hurry otherwise he might run off and kill himself because Ruth didn't get to the phone in time

RUTH: It's not him it's unknown *(Gives DANA a filthy look and answers.)* Hello

DANA: Oh for fuck's sake *(She sits down on the sofa and starts making herself a drink.)*

RUTH: Oh my god sorry yes hello, I didn't have your numb…

JESSICA: Dana *(She puts her arm around her.)*

RUTH: Sorry? What?

JESSICA: You know what fuck it, it was a mistake it doesn't matter

RUTH: What!

They all look over at RUTH, RUTH covers her mouth.

JIM: More histrionics

RUTH: You're…oh my god, how do you know…he said what…I'm, I'm coming, I'll come right now…okay, yes I know, okay, okay I'm coming…shit, yes, okay, coming

RUTH hangs up the phone.

JESSICA: What?

RUTH: That was his parents

JIM: 'Twix's'?

RUTH: He's in hospital he just, he just tried to kill himself

DANA: Oh

JESSICA: Jesus Christ

DANA: Fuck, is he okay?

RUTH: Well he's hit his head

DANA: What did he do?

RUTH: He, he was drunk and climbed up onto a bus shelter dived off it so he like landed on his head

JIM bursts out laughing he manages to stifle it quickly, JESSICA looks at him and gestures for him to go away, fist in mouth he gets up and leans on the sofa facing away from the girls, DANA and RUTH haven't noticed.

DANA: How do you know it wasn't an accident?

RUTH: He was shouting, he said he was going to kill himself

DANA: Where is he?

RUTH: St Thomas

DANA: Jesus are you going to go?

RUTH: Yeah

DANA: You want me to come?

RUTH: No that's okay, shit I better um…I need…

DANA: Okay look we'll get your bag and shoes and stuff

RUTH: 'Kay

DANA: Right come on

DANA takes RUTH's hand and leads her off down the corridor into her room, when JESSICA hears the door close she turns on JIM.

JESSICA: Can you stop being such a cunt for two minutes of your life?

JIM: Sorry, sorry

JESSICA: You come here and just fuck everything right up

JIM: Sorry your friends think you are boring or...

JESSICA: You know what I mean

JIM: What?

JESSICA: Earlier

JIM: What?

JESSICA: Fuck this

JIM: Oh of course everything is my fault! We have a fight...

JESSICA: It's not about the fight

JIM: Then what? Hm? What? *(JESSICA doesn't answer.)* You know not everything has to be a performance, not everything has to be some hysterical bloody Greek tragedy...

JESSICA: Then you want us never to talk about...

JIM: There is nothing to talk about? Talk about what?

JESSICA: Well there is either nothing to talk about or you don't know what I'm talking about?

JIM: *(Confused.)* What?

JESSICA: Because you just said that there is nothing *(Something in JIM's expression annoys her.)* Oh you know what; all it is is that you're a creepy little pervert so fucking unused to being near me that you don't think of me as your daughter you think of me as just the same as Ruth or Dana who you've been leching over all tonight

JIM: Is that what you really think?

DANA: *(From offstage.)* BBM me when you get to the hospital okay?

DANA and RUTH emerge from the corridor.

RUTH: Yeah sure

DANA: And you will be okay to get there?

RUTH: Yeah it's cool okay. Right I'll call you guys okay, bye

JESSICA: Bye, call us

RUTH: Okay see you

RUTH leaves, DANA shuts the door behind.

DANA: Fuck what a drama

SCENE SIX

6am. DANA is half asleep on the sofa, JIM is smoking a cigarette sitting in the cushions, JESSICA has a blanket around her and is sitting on the sofa arm she lights a cigarette.

JIM: Shall I turn the TV on?

JESSICA shrugs.

JIM: Music?

Shrugs again.

JIM: Now you're the one that isn't saying anything

JESSICA: Why does everyone like you?

JIM: What?

JESSICA: We're exactly the fucking same. But everyone's getting mad at me

JIM: We're not the same Jess

JESSICA: Dana wake up

DANA: Mm?

JIM: Let her sleep

JESSICA: No because I don't want to be on my own with you. Dana wake up

DANA: What? What's going on?

JESSICA: You were snoring

DANA: Well that's attractive. Where's, oh shit…

JESSICA: What?

DANA: I just remembered

JESSICA: What?

DANA: Everything *(DANA sits up.)* Oh Jesus when I came in did I brush my teeth?

JIM: Nope

DANA: Eurgh

DANA gets up and goes to the bathroom; you can hear her cleaning her teeth.

JIM: My mouth tastes like an ash tray

DANA: I feel really sick

JIM: We've drunk a lot. Do you want something to eat?

JESSICA: Please, private girls school we're taught to want 'Gucci' not food

DANA: No

JIM: Well I'm going to get some water if nothing else

JIM goes to the kitchen, DANA emerges from the bathroom.

DANA: Jess, what am I going to do?

JESSICA: What? *(Looks up at her, relents.)* Don't look so miserable, come sit down

JESSICA hugs DANA.

DANA: I've really fucked everything up

JESSICA: Tell me what happened, properly

DANA: Like we slept together and like he didn't, oh it was just disgusting I don't want to talk about it, it was just really gross and like you don't want to know it will put you off sex for life

JIM emerges he hasn't got water but more alcohol, he sees they are talking so goes back into the kitchen.

JESSICA: Did you use a condom?

DANA: No, I mean that doesn't matter I'm on the pill and whatever but it was just like, like eurgh and then he said at the end 'work's going to be tricky isn't it' and I said 'no it'll be fine Mr Tevers' then he was like 'maybe just don't come in' and at first I didn't get what he meant and it was so embarrassing because I was being so flirty and stuff but when I realised he was like sacking me I got so angry and he just like gave me some money and said 'redundancy package' and then like his fucking like flatmate came out, I didn't even know he had a flatmate and was like 'mate who's this' and he was like 'don't worry she's going'

JESSICA: What a cunt

DANA: You know what that doesn't help

JESSICA: Sorry

DANA: No I'm so fucking sick of coming home with these embarrassing stories and you all are like 'what a cunt you deserve better'

JESSICA: You do

DANA: No I don't I really don't

JESSICA: Oh don't be thick

DANA: I can't blame every guy for being a dick, it's my fault I'm a fucking slut and regret it every time. It was in my head even then when I left to see Ben and Ruth was trying to make me not go

JESSICA: Everyone makes mistakes

DANA: But not the same one again and again. I knew this
would happen!

JESSICA: That he would sack you?

DANA: No not that, that's just the fucking final fucking... Ah.
I hate this. I went and in my head I was thinking you are
going to regret this you are going to hate yourself and I just
went anyway

JESSICA: Why?

DANA: I don't know that's what I'm fucking saying! It's now
I'll feel bad about myself for a week until I find someone
else but now I haven't even got a fucking job I'm such a
waste of fucking space, I'm 22 what am I doing?

JESSICA: It's fine, you are in control...

DANA: No Jess you just, you just don't get it. You and Ruth
you both think that everyone is really like you they are just
pretending to be different but I'm not I'm not like you I'm
just some fucking idiot *(Diving into the sofa.)*

JESSICA: Look you just need to go to bed and then we'll go on
Gumtree and look for some jobs and...

DANA: You are so fucking practical you are like some
pragmatic fucking unemotional genius. You are like some
Vulcan

JESSICA: What the fuck is a Vulcan?

DANA: Fuck's sake

JESSICA: What the hell is a Vulcan?

DANA: In Star Trek Enterprise and the film there...

JESSICA: Oh for fuck's sake

DANA: They're these fuckers that don't show or have any
emotion

JESSICA: Oh well fuck me yeah maybe I…

JIM: *(Coming out of the kitchen still drinking.)* Yes fuck fuck fuck, don't you girls know any other words

DANA: Sorry but like Jess, Jim Jess is like some Vulcan thing I'm so fucking jealous. I'm just a slut and I should just admit it and enjoy it.

JESSICA: What Secret Diary of A Call Girl going to start right now in front of me

DANA: No but I mean okay whatever bad experience. I got a jumper out of it and a hundred quid

JESSICA: When did you get a jumper?

DANA: He gave me a jumper a few days ago

JESSICA: What?

DANA: The navy mohair one

JESSICA: You said you bought that

DANA: No well he bought it for me

JESSICA: Dana!

JIM: What's mohair from?

JESSICA: What?

JIM: Mohair?

DANA: I dunno

JIM: Mohair, hair of the mo?

> *DANA and JIM weakly laugh, keys at the door, someone can't open it they turn and look*

JESSICA: That Ruth?

DANA: Probably

JESSICA: Ruth?

RUTH: *(From behind the door.)* Yeah it's me, let me in will you

JESSICA: *(Going to the door.)* Where's your key?

RUTH: I can't fucking... *(RUTH opens the door almost hitting JESSICA in the face.)* Shit, sorry sorry the key, couldn't...Hi

DANA: You okay? How's Twix?

RUTH: Yeah, like, sorry the door

JIM: Hello sweetheart

RUTH: Hi, have none of you gone to bed?

DANA: Not really

RUTH: Fuck, God this has been such a crazy night

DANA: How's Twix? *(RUTH doesn't really respond is looking around.)* Oi Ruth how's Twix?

RUTH: Like, yeah he'll, yeah he's gonna be fine

DANA: Thank fuck

RUTH: Yeah, well like they were worried about like swelling or something I didn't really understand but he's just got a bad concussion they are keeping him in for a bit but yeah, his mum's there and she's a bitch so I just came home

JESSICA: But he'll be ok?

RUTH: Yeah...yeah

JESSICA: Thank god

DANA: Did you talk to him?

RUTH: A bit, well yeah like yeah

DANA: Did he say anything about why he, you know

JIM: *(Suppressing a snigger.)* Hurled himself off a bus shelter

JESSICA kicks him.

RUTH: Yeah he like explained how he was feeling and stuff. Like he has a thing about security and feeling in control and sometimes he freaks out about losing me. I mean it's all because of his mum and stuff. Like he had a really hard time when he was younger when his parents divorced I mean Dana you've heard him talk about that haven't you?

DANA: Mm

RUTH: And like he was always scared that he would be rejected by them and so when he thinks that I might be doing it to him he tries to hurt me so that he won't be the first one to be hurt

JIM: So he jumped off a bus shelter, flawless logic

RUTH: No well...

JESSICA: *(Hissing.)* Dad

RUTH: No he was hurting and was scared he'd lost the only person that meant anything to him and he just said he couldn't imagine...

JIM: Jesus...

JESSICA: Maybe you should stop drinking

RUTH: Like he tried to kill himself when he was younger like he cut his wrists because he felt trapped

JIM: So he wanted to set his blood free

RUTH: No like everyone was suppressing him and he said that I was just so different and that he'd never met anyone like me before so he is really worried about not being good enough for me

JIM: How long is this going to go on for?

JESSICA: Dad for fuck's sake

JIM: I'm sorry Ruth darling but really, really I can't, I can't just sit here and you're talking such pathetic bollocks

RUTH: I can't explain it right

JESSICA: Dad

JIM: No sweetheart you are explaining it just right I get it, just all you bloody kids so wrapped up in your self-made problems

JESSICA: Can you stop please? Stop fucking drinking and…

JIM: All of you thinking everything is so bloody serious and dramatic none of you have ever had a problem in your life

JESSICA: *(Trying to take the bottle off him.)* Yeah and fine dad you have experienced the damn holocaust

JIM: *(Pushing her roughly away and standing.)* Always fucking sarcastic. Ruth I know you are a nice girl but you and this bloody Twix object and even you Dana sulking over some little thing with some child, you are all such children

JESSICA: Dad you're drunk

JIM: And you Jessie, more than any of them. Grow up. Life is tough. Ok? Kids? You can't all sit around in the dregs moaning and poking about looking for some trauma or drama or cause. You are not special, you are not different, you are not unique and by the way I can tell you this Ruth you are not in love. You are a child, you're children in a little bubble and…

JESSICA: *(Trying to interrupt.)* Dad…

JIM: *(Coming closer and cutting her off.)* I know

JESSICA: Dad…

JIM: I know

JESSICA: Please…

JIM: I know *(Puts his hand over JESSICA's mouth.)* I'm, I am Jessie a spineless wasted coward or whatever it is you are wanting to say right now. But life screws you over. *(Turns back to RUTH.)* And if your poor troubled boyfriend has nicked his wrist or jumped off a damn bus shelter in some attempt to show his teenage hormone-fuelled passion big deal. No one cares. No one really cares and you caring just fuels the little self-absorbed drama you have all created. He is nothing special, you are nothing special, I am nothing special and no one is going to save you from that

JESSICA: *(Pushing him right away from her and he sits.)* Dad for fuck's sake what is…

JIM: The truth

JESSICA: Fuck that

JIM: And the truth will set you free girls

JESSICA: You're drunk

JIM: Yes I am

JESSICA: And feeling sorry for yourself about mum you don't have to drag everyone else down…

RUTH: Leave him alone Jess

JESSICA: What?

RUTH: You are fucking right Jim

JESSICA: He's pissed

RUTH: Who cares, what he is saying is right

JESSICA: You can't do this

RUTH: What?

JESSICA: Don't you dare do this

RUTH: What?

JESSICA: You can't just buy another load of crap from someone, not from him! Look at him for fuck's sake!

DANA: Jess don't be so mean

JESSICA: He's telling you not to like buy into all this shit but he just said his own load of bullshit

DANA: *(Appeasing.)* It wasn't bullshit

JESSICA: Of course it fucking was

RUTH: No it wasn't

JESSICA: You can't do this you just leapfrog to the next load of crap to buy into

RUTH: Leapfrog?

JESSICA: From another guy

RUTH: But he's right, Jesus Jess I am so jealous of you having a dad who…

JESSICA: Who what? Is a cunt?

RUTH: Jesus do you not understand okay? Truth is hard to hear but Jim you're right I have been self-centred and thinking I'm…

JESSICA: Stop it Ruth you are freaking me out. Dad please fucking stop this…

JIM: It's the truth

DANA: Jess you do the same what was with that stupid speech you did earlier about sex or something it's all bullshit, your dad is a clever bloke okay…

JESSICA: What! This is just some kind of stupid fucked up ball worshipping

DANA: What?

JESSICA: I swear to god if I was a guy you lot would think I was a genius as well. He's an about-to-be-divorced loser

JIM: Fiona won't divorce me

RUTH: Leave him be Jess why do you have to judge everyone

JESSICA: Okay look I can't stand this anymore he is nothing special

DANA: Jess stop it go to bed or something

JESSICA: No I won't go to bed, I fucking won't go to bed! Get out dad, Jim. Get the fuck out

JIM: What have I done?

JESSICA: I have put up with your crap all night and now you're not stopping this

RUTH: Stopping this?

JESSICA: Dad

JIM: You're throwing me out?

JESSICA: You've been mean, you've been judging, you've been patronising, you've been rude to me and my friends

JIM: Your friends can speak for themselves

RUTH: Yeah and he's been lovely

JIM: See?

DANA: Don't worry Jim, Jess go to bed obviously Jim doesn't have to leave

JESSICA: Yes he fucking does please dad, please just go, go away

DANA: No Jess go to bed, you go away it's fine

JESSICA: It's not fine please leave dad *(Mouthing to him.)* please

JIM: I've got nowhere to go

JESSICA: I don't care

JIM: You'd make me homeless

JESSICA: You've got a credit card haven't you? Stay in a hotel. You've got Auntie Sue? Stay with her

JIM: Sue has got three kids I can't just barge in

JESSICA: And you can't just barge in here, I don't want you here

JIM: You want me on some park bench

JESSICA: Don't be stupid, what do you want for me to beg?

DANA: Everyone's been drinking

JESSICA: I'm not drunk right now, he is, like you would notice being on a bench please just go, just get out

RUTH: Don't be stupid Jess! He's got nowhere to go

JESSICA: He's not a fucking child

JIM: I am here you know

JESSICA: That's the fucking problem isn't it?

RUTH: Well then why don't you go Jess?

JESSICA: What?

RUTH: You can stay with your mum and Barry, Jim can stay here until he is sorted out

JESSICA: This is my flat

RUTH: Yeah and mine and Dana's we can decide

JESSICA: Can you stop being so melodramatic I mean for fuck's sake you can't throw me out

DANA: Well Jess stop trying to throw Jim out

JESSICA: He's my dad I brought him here, I'm sorry I brought him here but I can get him to leave

JIM: Can you stop talking about me like I'm a dog Jessica

RUTH: You've been nothing but horrible to him all night

JESSICA: What are you even doing here Ruth? Shouldn't you be in the hospital with your precious boyfriend not here creating another little drama

RUTH: You are just disgusting you know that? I'm your friend and you talk to me like that?

JESSICA: He said worse

JIM: I know I know and I'm sorry Ruth I didn't mean to be cruel

RUTH: No I know

JIM: It's been a long night for us all and I'm still a bit on edge after everything with Fiona okay and I shouldn't have taken it out on you

RUTH: There was a lot of truth in what you said

JESSICA: He was talking shit

DANA: Come on Jess you've said all that stuff before behind her back

RUTH: Oh okay really?

JESSICA: Well now I see I should have been saying it to your face because it apparently would have made me a fucking oracle

RUTH: You know what I can't live with you anymore. Always fucking angry and complaining thinking you're some misanthrope who people gravitate toward or something but you are actually just a nasty little bitch

JESSICA: Ok fine don't live with me, then you get out. Go and jump off a bus shelter with your limp little waster green-haired boyfriend? You are a joke

RUTH: He hasn't got green hair anymore!

JIM: Girls calm down

DANA: Look Jess let's just leave it for tonight everyone's really upset

JESSICA: Oh it's the whore come to restore law and order I see

DANA: Oh you know what fuck you, fuck right off. Me and Ruth want you gone so fuck off

JESSICA: You can't do this

JIM: Jessie leave it for tonight maybe you should just go to your mum's

JESSICA: You could put a stop to this

JIM: You're upset

JESSICA: Please dad

JIM: I'm not leaving

JESSICA: Do you have to be so fucking pathetic? Stand up for me

JIM: Stop calling me pathetic

JESSICA: But you are, you are being a spineless fucking…

JIM: Right then I won't be, I won't be. But fuck standing up for you Jess, I'll stand up for myself. Get out go on get out

JESSICA: …my flat

JIM: And how many times have I helped you out with the rent?

JESSICA: Not for…

JIM: Earned myself one night I would think and Dana and Ruth don't want you here, so get out go to Fiona for the night I'm not making you homeless like you would me

JESSICA: Don't be stupid you wouldn't be fucking homeless

RUTH: Why do you even want to stay? If I'm so stupid and self-absorbed and your dad's so pathetic and Dana's a whore why you'd want to stay?

JESSICA: *(About to cry.)* Yeah, yeah you're right why would I?

RUTH: So fuck off

JESSICA grabs her coat and bag.

JESSICA: Where's my umbrella?

RUTH: I don't know do I?

JESSICA: It's fucking pouring I'm not going without it, I left it here

DANA: I borrowed it, sorry

JESSICA: Please can I have it back?

DANA: I, I um left it at Ben's

JESSICA: What?

DANA: Sorry

JESSICA: Fine so I'll just get soaked

RUTH: Fuck's sake *(Goes down the corridor.)*

DANA: What was it like a fiver, calm down

JESSICA: Fuck off

RUTH: *(Returning with an umbrella and giving it to JESSICA.)* Here fucking take that, are you going now

JESSICA: Fine, yes I am *(Pulling her coat on.)*

A phone rings.

JIM: *(To JESSICA.)* Aren't you going to answer that

JESSICA: It's not mine

JIM looks to DANA and RUTH, RUTH shakes her head and DANA gets out her phone.

DANA: It's not me

RUTH: It's you Jim

JIM: Oh is it? So unused to my mobile

RUTH: *(To JESSICA.)* Are you going or not?

JIM: Hello?

JESSICA: *(At the door about to leave.)* I don't…

JIM: Fiona? *(They all look at JIM on the phone.)* What? When did you…oh, oh Christ. Oh Jesus fucking Christ. Have you called…no? No? Okay well I better, yes well…? No! Don't let him anywhere near it Fiona. No, no, absolutely not… okay good… oh I see. I see. Well, I'll yes. Move whatever you can out and call, call Jay the number's in my diary in my study, better leave it till 8. Well hopefully will be back by then. Yes of course, of course. See you shortly. *(Ends the phone call.)*

RUTH: You're going?

JIM: Yes I've got to, emergency

DANA: Is everything okay?

JIM: The whole ceiling in the spare room has caved in

DANA: What?

JIM: That leak I mean for God's sake that's why we got Barry in in the first place…

DANA: She only threw you out yesterday

JIM: What's that got to do with my ceiling?

DANA: So she just called you at like 6.30 in the morning

JIM: Woke up to some almighty noise, went in water everywhere. Must have been leaking through into the attic for a while now, piling up behind those Christmas boxes, they'll be ruined too.

RUTH: So you're going back?

JIM: Yes I can't leave the water dripping through to the rest of the house, got to move all the stuff, get Jay over

RUTH: Who's Jay?

JIM: The builder

DANA: Why can't Barry do it?

JIM: I'm not letting that man touch the house! He's done enough damage! He was the roofer that's made a pig's ear of it in the first place

DANA: It's not your problem Jim

JIM: Of course it's my problem!

RUTH: But, but you've moved out

JIM: Yes, well probably not permanently, well I don't know. Look I must get my things I can't hang around here any longer *(Starts getting his stuff together.)*

RUTH: I don't understand

JIM: Look I have responsibilities, it's been a lot of fun, well a lot of hard work seeing all of you but a lot of fun. Thank you for letting me stay

RUTH: You shouldn't go running back whenever she clicks her fingers!

DANA: Yeah you can't just do whatever she says after everything

JIM: Look I know you're only trying to help. But after twenty six years of marriage it's not about playing silly little dating games where you 'don't do what your wife says'

RUTH: But she left you! She cheated on you

ANYA REISS

JIM: With a roofer who has just near gone and destroyed my
    house, I hate to think how much this is going to cost I will
    be having words with him

RUTH: This is fucking mad

JIM: No Ruth this is life, I mean grow up!

RUTH: Grow up?

JIM: This is adapting and dealing with the situation

RUTH: The situation?

JIM: I can't just hide in some little flat in London avoiding real
    life

RUTH: Avoiding real life?

JIM: Could you please stop repeating everything I'm saying
    dear

RUTH: But...How can you say hiding from real life! My
    boyfriend is in hospital...

JIM: Shall we not get back into that again! *(RUTH goes to speak.)*
    Now let's not leave on bad terms

DANA: She left you but you care more about the house

JIM: Well it actually cost rather a lot of money

RUTH: Stop being so patronising

JIM: Now don't get upset you've had a very long night no
    need for rudeness. It's all probably going to blow over now
    isn't it, you know the way Fiona is about the house Jessie
    probably going to see quite a battered Barry when I get
    there. Now girls very nice to see you

RUTH: Jim...

JIM: See you all soon hopefully, would say do it again but
    think my liver will need a good long break after this

DANA: You're really going?

JIM: 'Fraid so

DANA: This your click grow-up moment?

JIM: My what?

DANA: You said about growing up the moment when you're an adult

JIM: Did I? Been drinking rather a lot though now haven't we? Now see you all, bye bye Jessie now don't look at me like that you can stay now can't you? *(Gives her a clumsy hug which she doesn't respond to, at the door.)* Right um *(Checks with the cross action.)* Spectacles, testicles, wallet and watch *(Smiles, no response.)* Right well, see you all anon

JIM leaves and shuts the door, JESSICA faces the door and turns round to DANA and RUTH who go to the window to watch Jim leave, JESSICA sits on the sofa. DANA and RUTH see him leave they turn back round, long pause.

DANA: Drink?